Praise for *The Crazy Busy Cure*

'Don't mistake being busy for being productive! Zena Everett helps you understand what to do, and what to stop doing, and what parts of your schedule are just distractions. Create time to read this important book and start spending your time where it counts.'

– *Marshall Goldsmith, New York Times #1 bestselling author, two-time winner of the Thinkers 50 Award for #1 Leadership Thinker in the World, and #1 Executive Coach in the World*

'Chances are you're already wasting hours being busy without being productive. Take one or two of those hours to read this book. Follow its advice, and you'll get weeks of productive focus in return.'

– *Peter Bregman, bestselling author of* 18 Minutes *and* Leading with Emotional Courage

'Diving into our deep work is what makes life worthwhile in the end, but we all get distracted by curveballs, beeping phones, endless emails and sometimes our own procrastinating minds. I loved the *Crazy Busy Cure*'s ideas for getting out of our own way, saying NO to the myriad distractions and getting on with work that really makes a difference. That to me is very powerful indeed.'

– *Caroline Goyder, author of* Gravitas *and* Find Your Voice

'Zena is one of the most effective people I have ever worked with. She has a rare combination of knowledge, insight and pragmatism which makes her perfectly placed to write about productivity. If you want to get your professional life back under control, read this book.'

– *Dr Clare Gilbert Laurent, founding co-director of Shrink Technologies, and consultant and faculty member at School of Life*

'From my vantage point as a Non-Executive Director, I see executives derail because they get stuck in a blind tunnel of crazy busy working, leaving no time for strategic thinking or spotting opportunities. This book has no-nonsense ideas for protecting two of our most valuable resources: time and attention.'

– Paul Viner, Chief Financial Officer of Xstrahl and former Finance Director at Tottenham Hotspur PLC

'Smart management of time and energy is a requirement for all leaders building high performing organisations. Zena defines some actionable and really impactful steps to help us regain control of our time, our attention and focus. *The Crazy Busy Cure* is a must-read for all leaders.'

– Katie Danby, Chief Operating Officer for Wealth and Personal Banking at HSBC UK

'*The Crazy Busy Cure* is full of practical tips for responsible employers on allowing people to get on with their best work and feel great about themselves. Zena's Lawn Mower management concept reminds us that clearing the path to productivity should be the first priority of every successful manager.'

– Margaret Gooch, Human Resources Director at Brakes UK

'Business has been too busy for too long. People are amazing, but if we are bullied into working for much more than 30 hours a week, our productivity declines rapidly. In the UK, we have the longest working hours in Europe and yet the second-lowest productivity rate. Crazy business is not only irrational, it is immoral. Research is very clear that most people at work suffer damaging levels of stress, anxiety and (passive) aggression. This is why Zena Everett's *The Crazy Busy Cure* is so welcome given the opportunities we now have to build a better working world.'

– Roger Steare, The Corporate Philosopher

'Zena Everett's ideas are practical, purposeful, provocative and perfect if you want to be more productive, successful, happy and less busy.'

— Brendan Barns, founder of London Business Forum

'Lawyers battle with the need to track their hours whilst creating more time for what's truly important. This book enables us to work and live more efficiently, reconsidering our relationship with time.'

— Elaine O'Driscoll, Managing Partner of P.J. O'Driscoll & Sons LLP

'This book is a must-read to help busy professionals create uninterrupted blocks of time, feel in control of their day and work at their best.'

— Emma Crowley, Head of Legal Professional Training at McCann FitzGerald

'As a head-hunter I assess executives on their ability to think strategically and then execute. 24/7 demands on our time means the ability to manage our focus and attention is vital. This book should be on every leader's shelf.'

— David Goldstone, CEO of David Goldstone Associates

'Leading at scale and enabling your teams to be at their best to deliver value for customers means being at your best, focused on the critical priorities. The Crazy Busy Cure is "crazy good medicine" full of practical tips to cut through the constant clutter of distractions so you can think and innovate. That's where new possibilities are created!'

— Rod Wooten, Global Marketing Head of Pharma at Novartis

'Organizations following Zena's steps will see a measurable step-change in those key areas that boost productivity including motivation, happiness, innovation and ultimately delivery of business outcomes.'

– Vikki Osborne, Global Culture, Change Management and Future Capabilities Lead at Brambles

The Crazy Busy Cure

Zena Everett

The Crazy Busy Cure

A productivity book for people with no time for productivity books

Zena Everett

NICHOLAS BREALEY
PUBLISHING

London • Boston

First published by Nicholas Brealey Publishing in 2021
An imprint of John Murray Press
A division of Hodder & Stoughton Ltd,
An Hachette UK company

This paperback edition published in 2022

1

Copyright © Zena Everett 2021

A CIP catalogue record for this title is available from the British Library

Paperback ISBN 978 1 529 36709 6
Trade Paperback ISBN 978 1 529 36708 9
eBook ISBN 978 1 529 36710 2

Typeset by KnowledgeWorks Global Ltd.

Printed and bound in Great Britain by Clays Ltd, Elcograf S.p.A.

John Murray Press policy is to use papers that are natural, renewable and recyclable products and made from wood grown in sustainable forests. The logging and manufacturing processes are expected to conform to the environmental regulations of the country of origin.

John Murray Press
Carmelite House
50 Victoria Embankment
London EC4Y 0DZ

Nicholas Brealey Publishing
Hachette Book Group
Market Place, Center 53, State Street
Boston, MA 02109, USA

www.nicholasbrealey.com

Through discipline comes freedom

Aristotle

Contents

How certifiably Crazy Busy are you?

How many of these apply to you?

- ☐ You have so much to do that you can't get anything done.
- ☐ You over-commit and find it hard to say no.
- ☐ You are always 'on', connected, but deep down you feel disconnected from the people that matter to you.
- ☐ Your colleagues, friends and family often say how busy you seem.
- ☐ You can barely find time to think, never mind think strategically.
- ☐ You feel that you fit your own needs and priorities around the sides of everyone else's.
- ☐ You spend the least amount of time on the one priority that would have the greatest potential impact. This really bugs you, but you can't sort it out.
- ☐ You also have an idea of something which feels like a real game-changer, but you haven't got time to figure it out.
- ☐ Your calendar is full of meetings. You don't have time to switch from one to the other or prepare properly.
- ☐ Email is the bane of your life. Your inbox has become your to-do list.
- ☐ You've more or less given up on getting anything meaningful done during 'normal' working hours because you are interrupted so often.
- ☐ If you manage others, chances are your team is under-resourced. They sometimes miss deadlines and say they have too much to do. Other managers are starting to complain that your team cause bottlenecks.
- ☐ You feel guilty when you delegate to busy people. Team tasks aren't evenly distributed: your best people get the most to do and your underperformers get away with it.

☐ You rarely eat lunch at lunchtime and usually graze in front of a screen.

☐ You like to fix things for other people and make their life better. It's important to you that people like you.

☐ On the rare occasions you get some free time, you fill it up. You can't remember ever thinking 'what shall I do today?'

☐ You take criticism personally and have been told you are over-sensitive. You hate making mistakes.

☐ Sometimes you struggle to get on with your work because you just aren't in the mood.

☐ You get anxious if you don't respond to emails or texts immediately.

☐ You are rarely in the mood to concentrate on 'deep' work so put off those jobs until you are in the mood or are up against a deadline.

☐ Life feels overwhelming and you have a sense that it's passing you by. It's certainly not as much fun as it used to be.

☐ LinkedIn depresses you. Other people have achieved so much more.

☐ Work feels like the gym – you peddle furiously but never move forwards. (And you never get to the gym.)

☐ You didn't read this list properly. You just skimmed through it, like you read everything.

Results: Just how certifiably Crazy Busy are you?

I'm not going to score this like one of those magazine quizzes I adored when I was a teenager. You know the type:

- **Over twenty ticks:** Cardiac arrest waiting to happen. Your crazy busyness has got so bad that you are about to combust.

- **Over ten ticks:** Tail-chaser. Your career is going nowhere because you are so inefficient.

- **Under ten ticks:** Chancer. What do you actually do all day? You are lucky you've held onto your salary this far without being rumbled as a total malingerer.

And so on. I'm keeping this light-hearted, but the addiction to busyness, this busy sickness, isn't funny at all.

If you've ticked the very first question, that's enough. If you feel that you have so much to do that it is hard to get anything done, then, like too many of us in twenty-first century organizational life, you are Crazy Busy.

How Crazy Busy you feel is your business. My business is to get you off this competitively busy, lonely busy, crazy busy bandwagon. You'll be more successful and happier too.

The first step in curing you is that you decide that the way you work isn't working for you anymore. It's probably not working for your organization either. What are the consequences for your life and career if you keep spinning around like this?

If you can achieve your real work more efficiently, you will get your job done in reasonable hours. It's that simple. You can clock off, have a life, spend time with people you value, do something you enjoy, re-energize, breathe, maybe even have time to put some of your hard earned cash back into the economy. You will be more productive and fulfilled and so will the people you work with.

Most important of all, you will control what you choose to do all day: my definition of success.

Who do you want to be?

CRAZY BUSY PERSON	HAPPY PRODUCTIVE PERSON
Hard worker	High performer
Lost in busyness	Does the business
Mired in the weeds	Operates strategically
Fires off late night emails	Sleeps on a problem and emails thoughtfully
Always rushing with no time to talk	Projects a calm aura, makes space to listen
Allows problems to escalate	Nips problems in the bud
Likes to please other people	Likes to please their Manager
Procrastinates	Does first things first
Dislikes difficult conversations	Encourages feedback
Long, out-of-date to-do list	Daily list of priorities, maximum three
Can't say no, always runs out of time	Prioritizes own goals and aligns these with organizational agenda
Popular colleague but has a reputation for slowing down projects because of their busyness	Always asked to join projects, often to lead the team
Calendar is full of back-to-back meetings, no time to prepare	Chooses meetings judiciously and prepares properly for them
Checks up on workers on shared projects	Checks in on progress of the workflow
Misses deadlines	Makes daily incremental progress
Feels overwhelmed	Feels in control
'Where's the week gone?'	'What do you need from me?'

Introduction

Crazy Busyness destroys productivity and happiness

What gets in your way of getting things done?

I am an executive coach. I realized early on that, regardless of their talent or ambition, one of the greatest success factors for my clients was how they focused their time and attention.

The way most of us spend our time at work isn't really working for us at all. We crash from one stultifying meeting to another, juggling multiple projects, receiving incessant emails, over-promising and under-delivering because there aren't enough hours in the day to get everything done. We are fixated on creating and hitting deadlines, one-upping each other on who is busier.

We run on autopilot, responding to last-minute demands, rarely pausing to question what to do next. We're lost in a rabbit hole of time and effort on tasks that, in the great scheme of things, don't make much difference. They feel like work, but they aren't really productive.

To add to the overwhelm, we are rarely offline. Our phones are practically taped to our hands. We can't bear to feel that we are missing out.

Test it for yourself. When you make a drink, can you just stand quietly with your own thoughts, or do you check your alerts? If you are in the car alone, waiting at the lights or stuck in a jam, do you have to fight every fibre in your being not to check your messages?

And when do you find time to think? That's what you are paid for after all – your thoughts, ideas, knowledge, experience, mental energy.

Our attention is so fragmented, it's hard to tune out the noise and focus.

In the last ten minutes, what did you pay attention to? Did you look up from this book. What's distracted you? What tried to get your attention? Where did your mind wander off to?

Even choices that should be pleasurable, like food, have become a minefield of cognitive overload. Brian Wansink and his team at Cornell University explored 'mindless autopilot' about what we eat and estimated we make over 226 daily decisions on food alone. These might seem mindless, but they still take up brainpower and add to the stress-inducing pace of our lives.

Just take the palaver of buying your morning coffee.

> *Yes, just ordinary milk please. Yes, just a medium size. No, I don't want anything with it. Yes, to take away. Z E N A, no just one E, not an X, a Z, oh no don't worry, X is fine. Thank you. Yes. I'll have a good day, you too, is this mine? Oh sorry, no, that's his, this is mine. Great. Thank you.*

Is this evolutionary progress? Life has speeded up but these encounters certainly don't spark joy; they feel slightly tense to me. I'm sure it's not pleasant for the server on the other side of the counter either, no matter how many badges and big smiles they are wearing.

Yet most of us adapt and survive our daily grind. Some of us thrive on it. As our level of responsibility increases, so do the number of choices we need to make and the plates we have to juggle. Who helps us to navigate this?

Being more productive doesn't mean working longer hours. It means choosing tasks with the greatest impact and then eliminating interruptions so that you can get on with them.

No one explains how to do this. We have to work out for ourselves how to ruthlessly prioritize, focus our attention only on work that matters, manage time into clusters of similar activities, stop trying to please everyone and, hardest of all, to say no.

Some of our busyness is at an organizational level too: I call this *cultural* busyness.

You know that tedious report you write every week that you suspect no one actually reads? Or the complex processes that duplicate effort just because 'we've always done it this way'? That's what I'm talking about, the mad stuff.

We battle with the 24/7 demands that digitization has created. The economist John Maynard Keynes made a joyous prediction back in 1930 that, by now, the working week would be drastically cut to about 20 hours a week. Workers would enjoy more leisure time and spend their material gains. Really?

Quite the opposite has happened.

We have loaded fake, busy work on top of real work.

Digitization has revolutionized how we work but created a whole layer of fake work on top of the real work. Most of us are knowledge workers. Compared to production line workers with a physical output, we produce non-tangible outcomes, like a spreadsheet or slide deck. Production lines are far more efficient than most head offices. We don't seem to appreciate the value of our talented human resources. Imagine if you were putting the wheels on a racing car, and then were told, stop that, just pop round the back and fix the exhaust, and then stop the line and have a meeting about it for a couple of hours?

That's how we work in most offices — constantly switching from one channel or screen or task to another and never counting the cost.

Consequently, we work longer hours than ever before to catch up on what we haven't done. Productivity rates are declining, so clearly that strategy doesn't work. We've all sorts of explanations/excuses but inefficiency is right up there.

With duplicated processes, clunky communication between teams, systems that aren't fit for purpose and inadequate training, it certainly feels like it takes longer to get some tasks done now than it did five or even ten years ago.

We are all increasingly sick, tired, lonely and frustrated.

Crazy Busyness makes us stressed, tired, wired. The last thing most of us do at night, and the first thing we do in the morning, is check our phone.

This is *connected* busyness. It's not real social connection. Deep down we know it. Powerful algorithms lure us back to social platforms, distracting us from our own priorities and interrupting our daily structure.

The damage caused by social media to our mental health, global political stability and efficiency is widely accepted. We are too wired to wake up to it. When did you last use your phone to have a deep conversation with someone?

Work can be isolating if you and all around you don't have time to listen to each other and build real connections. This is particularly hard if you are working remotely, but it's not guaranteed if you are in an office. Does your boss really understand who you are and what you want out of life? Do you know it yourself?

Good social relationships are the best indicator of how happy we will be. Whether you are working in isolation or in a busy team, our crazy busy schedules make it harder for us to build real connections in and out of work.

Networks play a critical part of career success, but the consequences of not having strong connections are much more frightening than mere career stasis.

Social-connectedness expert Julianne Holt-Lunstad conducted a trail-blazing meta-analysis of more than 3.4 million participants. It showed that social isolation and loneliness are linked with about a 30 per cent higher risk of early death. Her research on the links between social connectivity and mortality showed that people with strong social bonds are 50 per cent less likely to die over a given period of time than those who have fewer social connections.

Loneliness carries the same health risk as smoking 15 cigarettes a day.

We have to stop rushing because we are getting nowhere fast. We need to slow down, listen, build connections, prioritize and choose our activities more thoughtfully.

I'm a reformed Crazy Busy person

About 20 years ago I was approached by a TV production company making a programme about the seven deadly sins. They filmed a day in my life as the uptight antithesis of the sin of sloth: a headless chicken. The crew chased after me as I rushed around London, totally out of synch with myself and the rest of the world in the mindless pursuit of my goals.

I could never bring myself to watch the programme – too toe-curlingly embarrassing for words. I've no idea what the sloth chap did. I assume he spent most of his waking hours on the sofa but who knows what he was thinking about or what he went on to achieve after he pressed pause for a bit.

Now I'm a leadership coach. I help my clients to bridge the gap between where they are now and where they want to get to. This book is what I've learnt from curbing my own Crazy Busy triggers and thousands of hours coaching other people. If I can do it, you can too.

Goals are meaningless if you can't find time to start them.

Time and time again ambitious, talented clients would tell me that, despite their best intentions, they struggled to get impactful work done. They were frustrated about it. They'd come to work, usually clear on what they needed to get done that day, but would end up spending hours on routine admin, dealing with interruptions, distractions and curveballs (you know, 'can you just...'). Their working days extended as they sneaked in early in the morning to find some quiet time or stayed later every day to start work on whatever it was they had hoped to get done first thing. We are kidding ourselves if we think that the working day ended when they shut down their computer; those contracted hours are irrelevant. They were checking emails at night and first thing in the morning, sometimes in between. They often fired off late night emails, adding to the vicious circle. They were continually 'on' and making others continually on too.

I'd ask them to list the projects or initiatives that would have the most significant impact on their organization and career. Then we'd work out how much time they actually spent on them. Invariably they'd say that they spent the least amount of time on their main priorities and sometimes no time at all on the ones with the greatest potential.

Their reasons varied. They couldn't create a chunk of time to start the task, they didn't know how to start it and hadn't set aside time to figure out what that first step should be, or they delayed starting because they were afraid of a less than perfect outcome.

Procrastination is usually a big indicator of perfectionism and most high achievers have perfectionist tendencies. Most suffer from student syndrome too: leaving things right up to a deadline. If there is only an arbitrary deadline then it's easy to be distracted and delay starting. In all cases, they had little spare capacity. Their diaries were always clogged with meetings and they were constantly interrupted by their bosses and team so had no time to think. They were Crazy Busy.

Even worse were the *competitively* Crazy Busy ones. These boasted about being in back-to-back meetings like it's a badge of honour: 'I'm always rushing, therefore I am really important and indispensable.' They over-promised and under-delivered because they couldn't keep up with what they intended to do. They infuriated their colleagues.

What's the impact of your Crazy Busyness on others?

Crazy Busy people get promoted quickly because they are so good at executing the work. They are well-intended but poor managers. They aren't role models for how to work or what to aspire to. They don't have time to manage: to spot problems early on, to course-correct, to build trust, to listen to their team, to have career conversations. All they seem to do is to follow an HR guideline to have perfunctory weekly or fortnightly 1:1s with their teams.

I'm sure this all sounds familiar to you. Let's assume that everyone comes to work to do a good, honest job and then goes home to have a fulfilled life. We don't start our careers wanting to over-extend like this.

This book will unpick how our own driven personalities collude with digitization and badly managed organizational cultures to create this cocktail of unproductive, unhealthy Crazy Busyness.

What's happened to life outside work?

How many of us do much outside work apart from some sort of exercise, watching our multiple screens and scraping together a just-about-good-enough social and family life? It's a golden age of film and TV and there are so many demands for our attention. We are rarely bored, but our digital distractions deplete our energy levels.

I ask my audiences what they do in the evenings. Too many people tell me that they are so tired they can't be bothered to go out, to work out, or to cook a proper meal from scratch. They just flop in front of a screen, like they do all day at work, and graze. Or they have an equally Crazy Busy schedule outside work because they can't bear unstructured time. Their children's calendars are full too. Some of my friends are so booked up we have to use a doodle poll to fix a dinner date.

The really sad part is when I ask them what they would do if they had an extra hour in the day completely to themselves. They often don't know. They've lost touch with what makes them happy.

Why is it so difficult to snatch some precious time for ourselves? Clients often tell me they'd give anything for just one extra hour's sleep, but go to bed later than they should because they want time to decompress. The last thing they look at is a screen, but they know they need to get away from their screens. The media companies compete for our attention and defeat our craving to switch off and sleep. Keynes would be horrified by the compromises we make.

How can we get off this Crazy Busy bandwagon? We would never waste any other resource in the way we waste our time. Ironically it's a resource we can't recreate – once that precious hour is gone, it's gone for good.

This book is about regaining control of your time, attention and focus. If you are a leader, managing attention and focus is a huge and often unacknowledged challenge. I'll help you to crack it.

We'll also look at the impact of your crazy busy behaviours on your colleagues, especially meetings, emails, workflow management and giving feedback. Are you a sucker for all the instant messaging tools eagerly bought by your IT department keen to put this initiative on their LinkedIn profile, regardless of whether they improve communication or not? We'll stop that.

We are wasting talent

I believe it is an organizational responsibility to address this burden of busyness. They will reap productivity, profitability, engagement, well-being and retention gains from reconfiguring what their teams do all day. That's a far more effective intervention than all the costly initiatives they invest in now.

Great managers are rare. Organizations prioritize 'leadership' development over the nuts and bolts of management, delegation, feedback and resource planning skills. Expensive strategic thinking skills are pointless if leaders don't have the time to think. Well-being interventions like mindfulness training backfire if a hundred more emails are screaming at you when you return to your desk.

We all lose at least 20 per cent of our week on distractions and interruptions.

In 2017, Michael Mankins and Eric Garton of Bain and Co published a seminal book called *Time, Talent and Energy*. They describe 'organizational drag' – how we can lose up to 20 per cent of our time on all these institutional factors I've described that slow things down. Managers can lose up to 25 per cent and, to be clear, this isn't on properly managing their teams – it's from being pulled in different directions by multiple hi-jackers. Why hire the best talent and then get in their way?

Leaders aren't leading, giving us a vision and inspiring us to do great things. They are doing routine administration, meaningless tasks with very little, if any, significance.

If we can fix all this, that will help you to reclaim the equivalent of a day a week. What difference would that make to you?

Once you admit you are on this unproductive, energy sapping, sick-making, Crazy Busy headlock, it's possible to jump out of it. The solutions lie mostly with you, making better choices about what you do next. We have to spend our days in a more productive and meaningful way, instead of responding to what's screaming out in front of us, even if that's your disorganized boss.

My aim is to give you pragmatic steps to stop losing that 20 per cent of your time. Let's get you doing an honest day's work, feeling you've made progress. Then you can go home, have a life, spend your money to share the benefits of it and come back to work the next day restored of energy, focus and creativity.

It's the twenty-first century, that shouldn't be too much to ask should it? A YouGov survey of British workers found that 37 per cent of employees thought their job made no meaningful contribution to the world at all. That's heart-breaking.

Has COVID-19 rebooted our productivity?

The world is different since COVID-19. The crisis has forced us to change how we work and connect. Firms who track productivity say that we get more done virtually, because we aren't constantly interrupted. A long-needed wake-up call.

For the foreseeable future, we will be working apart at least some of the time. Businesses are rethinking their physical office requirements. Collaboration and brain storming are best done together in the office and we'll go home to focus on more detailed activities.

Good leaders upped the ante on their main touch points of virtual meetings and one-to-ones. They built trust with sensitive enquiries into people's wellbeing and personal circumstances. They gave shorter, easier deadlines to maintain motivation and communication. They say: 'I can't see if you are having a bad day so I need you to tell me.' Poor leaders just shifted their usual meeting schedule online, didn't check in enough with their teams and assumed that people will ask for help.

Leaders should see the lockdown experience as an opportunity to work smarter and more intensively, moving the focus firmly on results, not presenteeism.

Sadly, far too many of my clients work even longer hours when they are at home, without the boundaries of a commute. It's the 'just one more thing...' mentality. Some manage teams in different time zones and seem to me to have set up completely unsustainable working patterns.

I tell them that, whilst they are exceptionally clever and talented (they are), they are not super-human. Their body tells them that too. I've had more ill clients than ever: migraines, backache, stiff joints and digestive problems especially. I'm not a doctor but those seem like worrying indicators of stress to me.

How are you going to change?

Let's get you off this crazy busy bandwagon and make you a happy, productive person instead.

If you are saying 'yes' to this, then you are going to have to start saying 'no' too. You can't juggle all those plates. How will you prove your value, if you've always relied on being first online and last out to illustrate it? You might also have to curb your desire to control everything, please everyone and be perfect. That might have got you here, it won't get you to the next stage of responsibility when you simply have too many priorities to juggle.

Let's start by going back to basics and look at the root of your crazy busyness. We can't turn the clock back, but once we understand where a problem starts, it makes the solution more obvious.

PART 1

Diagnosis

CHAPTER 1

How you became hooked on Crazy Busyness

• • •

- Have you always prided yourself on being a hard worker?
- Were you brought up to believe that 'if a job's worth doing it's worth doing well'?
- Has anyone ever called you a workaholic?

Please don't beat yourself up for being Crazy Busy. It usually comes from very positive intentions and often serves as a defence mechanism.

It's likely that your work ethic and high standards have catapulted you into a successful career. Unless you recalibrate how you operate, these standards become a problem when the pressure of work means it is impossible to maintain them. You have to relinquish some control over your own impossibly high standards. This probably makes you feel very uncomfortable.

All strengths, when overused, have a shadow side. The traits and behaviours that put you on the fast track become detrimental.

Even if you decide to stay low down the corporate ladder, Crazy Busyness doesn't make you happy. You wouldn't be reading this book if it wasn't a problem.

In the words of best-selling executive coach and author Marshall Goldsmith:

> *What got you here, won't get you there.*

Crazy Busy people usually have one or more personality traits that have developed a shadow side: which is most like you?

1 YOU NEED TO BE PERFECT

If we go back to school days, you probably got praised for working really hard. You may or may not have been cleverer than most but actually this doesn't matter so much. Intelligence is a predictor of academic success, but there is limited correlation between IQ and success in the workplace (Richardson and Norgate, 2015). We all know people with extraordinary ambition and drive who get way further in life than their teachers predicted.

You could also have been rewarded for perfect performance. Nowadays parents are taught to praise and reward their kids for effort, which is under their control, rather than grade achievement, which isn't. You can't always control the end result.

Like most of their generation, however, my parents praised results and pushed for excellence. They focused on the one spelling I got wrong, not the 19 I got right.

I vividly remember one comment from my school reports. It was from my singing teacher: 'Zena could look happier when singing.' (In truth he was being enormously tactful as I can't hold a note.) However, my mother was so incensed about this 'ruining' my otherwise tiptop report that she rang the Headmaster to complain.

What did I learn from this? Life is binary – 100 per cent perfect or 100 per cent failure. No grey. I was tough on myself and focused on the deficit, never the positives. If I got 20/20 on spellings one week, I'd dismiss it as an easy test.

Perfectionists like me deliver perfect results but, of course, as we get more responsibility, we can't do everything perfectly anymore. That stresses us out. We aren't in control anymore. We prioritize low-value easier tasks, which we can control perfectly, over high-impact important ones. To delay a potentially less-than-perfect performance, we procrastinate. Plenty on procrastination later, as long as I don't run out of time.

As we try to keep doing all our tasks perfectly, we become whirling dervish Crazy Busy people, lost in the detail, with over-committed impossible diaries and unachievable to-do lists. Our busyness also stops us facing up to aspects of our lives we aren't so happy with.

Where perfectionists really hit the skids is that we can't bear criticism. We take feedback really hard, so we don't seek it out. Careers get derailed when we can't ask for help on our blind spots. As we advance into leadership roles, these blind spots are less about skills and more about our relationships with other people, trying to manage their productivity as well as our own.

In one of my favourite leadership books, *The Right and Wrong Stuff*, Professor Carter Cast of Kellogg School of Management explains that this defensiveness stops us learning and developing. It is a common reason why people's careers plateau.

2 YOU LIKE TO DO THINGS YOURSELF, RATHER THAN TRUST OTHERS

You are super strong on execution – the ability to get things done. You are a high performer, trusted to do a good job, to hit targets and work on your own initiative. You take on more responsibilities than your peers, work longer hours and push yourself to do well. You aren't frightened to get your hands dirty. This reputation is how you built your career and got promoted. No task is too small for you to put your hands up for and excel at.

Success at work comes first from our intrapersonal skills: our character traits and ability to manage ourselves. You are high in motivation, discipline, drive and ambition, but lower in focus, prioritization and organization skills.

As well as intrapersonal skills we also need interpersonal skills: our ability to work with other people and influence them to our point of view. Managing others means you have to get results *through* other people.

Crazy Busy people don't have the time to slow down and listen, to take people with them. They often are so focused on delivering the numbers that they don't have time to lift their head above the parapet and think strategically. They work from the detail up, because that's where they feel safe, sometimes missing the big picture altogether.

I coached a supply chain manager, Alessandro. He accelerated early in his career because of his outstanding negotiation tactics and forensic knowledge of each contract. But as a leader, he got very poor engagement scores from his team.

It turned out that they were burdened with several time-consuming projects that didn't justify the effort required in getting them off the ground. Even worse, some of the projects actually conflicted. This is classic cultural Crazy Busyness. The people on the ground knew it, but Alessandro wasn't listening to them.

When he finally paused to listen, the problem was obvious. 'What are we trying to achieve here' was all it took to prioritize some projects, shelve the rest and rebuild momentum.

Crazy Busyness gets in the way of career success. You can, of course, choose to come off the management track and continue as an individual contributor or subject matter expert. But dream on. You'll always have to influence and collaborate with other people. You can't be a bottleneck.

You'll get more and more overwhelmed. You might even reject career opportunities because you assume that they will make you even more tired.

3 YOU PUT OTHERS' NEEDS BEFORE YOUR OWN

Most of the Crazy Busy people I coach are exceptionally kind, nice people. They naturally gravitate towards management roles. They often end up involved in good causes, whether in their professional role, some side initiative or in a voluntary capacity.

Inevitably, they have taken on caring responsibilities early in life too, looking after parents or siblings who weren't able to take appropriate care of themselves, or perhaps were just unusually demanding.

Pleasing people at all costs, subjugating our needs to others, becomes a habit. In some cases, it's a survival mechanism. This was my situation, both my mother and father had physical and mental ill health. I always felt that I was responsible for my parents, not the other way around.

The world relies on people like us. That's what we tell ourselves anyway.

It's no coincidence that many coaches, therapists, medical professionals – anyone who helps others for a living – have had early caring responsibilities. This becomes our reality and we recreate this in our adult lives. That's the message we internalize about how the world works and our purpose in it.

The problem is we then take on more and more and can't cope with all the demands. We don't have boundaries.

Co-dependent people try to make things better for everyone else, even when that's impossible or unwanted.

Are you the person who remembers everyone's birthdays, who stays late to finish other people's work, who volunteers for projects that you don't really want to do, who even collects the cups at the end of each meeting? Do you feel resentful that your caring isn't appreciated or reciprocated? Are you praised for your hard work but overlooked for promotion? Do you get stressed easily and sometimes need to take time off? Do you do all the chores at home too? And feel guilty if you don't run the Parents' Association at your kids' school?

I'm not qualified to give a clinical psychological diagnosis, but I'd say this is a pretty likely indicator of a co-dependent personality type.

Co-dependent people are always looking for approval but are not good at asking for what they need. Asking for feedback is a big topic in this book, because feedback keeps our performance and productivity on track. Co-dependent people are hypersensitive to critical feedback so avoid asking for it.

Their identity is often tightly embedded into how well they do their job, so they find it hard to be rational when things don't go well. Stumbles are inevitable and, actually, to be encouraged because we all know that the best lessons come from mistakes. Co-dependents can't bear failure. They catastrophize: 'That presentation wasn't very good, so my entire life is a disaster.' Rather than take the risk of less-than-excellent performance, they stay well within their comfort zone, repeating crazy busy low-risk, low-value tasks that keep them psychologically safe.

Their mantra is 'what can I do for you?' and they are happy to work away behind the scenes. Savvy colleagues take advantage of this, making sure they get the credit, obviously referencing their colleague in their thank-you speech. They always want you in your team, even taking you with them when they move on. This fuels your need to be liked and helpful.

Hell, some of us were even taught by the system that co-dependence is the right way to behave.

When I was a Brownie, many years ago in Bandon, West Cork, Ireland, we were told about helpful little elves that snuck into the house when everyone was asleep, did all the chores, laid the fire (I told you it was a long time ago), made the breakfast and then flew away before anyone saw them. That's what young girls were encouraged to be like – to never demand thanks for good deeds, to be passive and selfless. Our rewards would come, but not if we asked for them.

Those types of messages stick in our subconscious minds until we boot them out when we are sick of being trampled over.

Please, wake up and smell that coffee you've just made for yourself, and probably everyone around you too.

Dial down your urge to over-extend and dial up your boundaries.

In her book *Co-dependent No More*, Melody Beattie suggests asking 'what do you need from me?' instead of 'what can I do for you?' It's a subtle shift but it means you aren't taking on the problem, just offering appropriate support. Try it yourself, it really works.

Now we know the roots of your Crazy Busyness. You can just blame your parents. Or you can take control by challenging the thinking errors that are the root of it. But maybe you feel that there isn't a psychological cause, that you just can't get on top of your workload. There's one more category to consider.

4 YOU STRUGGLE WITH ORGANIZATIONAL SKILLS, DESPITE YOUR BEST INTENTIONS

Perhaps you simply feel overwhelmed and struggle to get organized. Maybe you take on too much, or your boss makes everything too complex, or you just faff around rather than getting on with your work. This book contains intensely practical tools to tackle the people and processes that get in your way. You can control a lot more than you think.

And if, like me, you get lost easily, loathe spreadsheets and struggle with tedious detail, then maybe there is something else going on. Planning and processing is harder for us then it appears to be for others. Chapter 16 is for people with hidden processing problems like this, such as dyspraxia. I'll suggest coping strategies and hopefully give you the confidence to ask for more support.

So read on, to be cured.

First, we need data. Where does your day go?

CHAPTER 2

What eats up your time?

• • •

- Do you know how long it actually takes to do your job?
- What's got to go in order to create time to do what's important?

Why is it so hard to get anything done?

Crazy Busy people are 'process facilitators, shifting things along an invisible assembly line but without time to create something meaningful. High performers create something that's not there'. (Carter Cast again).

Coaches like me will tell you that in order to get promoted you need to take on extra responsibilities at the level you aspire to next. Don't wait for the opportunity to be given to you, start taking it now. Put your hand up, be visible and so on.

That's all well in principle, but what we don't tell you is how to find the time to do this extra added-value contribution. You are already maxed out. Adding on hours to your day is not a long-term solution. Whilst sometimes we have to lean in and work crazy hours (and that can be fun) there is zero evidence that working longer hours makes us more productive.

There's also no correlation between long hours and career success. Most of us are measured on quality of output, not quantity. The days are long gone when the person that stayed the longest in the office got promoted.

I earn my own living through selling my time. I charge for coaching sessions which are usually between 90 to 120 minutes. However, if my client achieves their lightbulb moments before that I don't drag out the session – we're done. They don't pay me for turning up, they pay me to facilitate their thinking. It's all about value.

You should be able to do a great job, in reasonable hours, then go home, have a life and return to work the next day as your very best self. That shouldn't be a big ask.

How many hours do you actually work?

I have lost count of the number of times people tell me that they are fulfilling their own (outdated) job description, covering for someone else because the team is a person short, whilst holding the fort for someone on sick leave. Then they volunteer to be on a Committee to make them look good. The numbers just don't add up! Something has to go; time is finite.

Ingrid, an audit senior, returned to work from maternity leave and dropped to a three-day week. Her billable hours target remained the same as when she was full-time. With a beautiful irony for an Economics graduate and chartered accountant, she never did the maths. Perhaps she just avoided the difficult conversation because she was 'grateful' to have a role to return to.

The workplace is no respecter of martyrs – assertiveness and negotiation skills are far more highly valued then a boundless capacity for being a doormat.

First-time managers, especially, end up working more hours than they should. You know the scenario – you do well at your job, so congratulations, you are promoted to team leader and given a completely unskilled newbie or two to manage. There's rarely a pragmatic conversation with your own boss about how to delegate or how to do your own job more efficiently. Instead you just stay later and later trying to catch up. You'll never get everything done and have to learn to live with that.

What has to go?

Until you drill down into what you really do with your time, it's just a fantasy to think you can squeeze more into your week, never mind complete everything on your list. What should you do and what's got to go?

Here's my Head Space Model. It tells you:

- What you do all week
- Where your extra Head Space comes from.

Head Space is the space that outstanding careers are built on. It is the time to handle new projects, think strategically, learn something new, have career conversations, build relationships, win awards, win business, get back in the weeds to fix a problem before it escalates, do research, remain a subject matter expert and so on. It's where you add a game-changing contribution. It is the antithesis of Crazy Busyness.

HEAD SPACE = TIME AVAILABLE − CORE JOB + CURVEBALLS + ROUTINE ADMIN

Head Space Model for diagnosing where your time goes

Time Available: How many hours do you have available to work each week?

Core Job: How long does it take to fulfil your job description? Ideally, you should know this and include the information in inductions/hand overs: 'when you are up to speed it should take 90 minutes to input those purchase orders', and so on.

This is a rare conversation, unless you are working to billable hours/timesheets. Even then, it's often a hazy calculation at best. Time and Motion studies are deemed to be old fashioned (I discuss Taylorism in Chapter 14 on mood).

Curveballs: These are all the 'can you just ...' extras that predictably come your way – how much time should you allow for these in a typical week?

Routine admin: This is all the small stuff that sucks up your time. Include minutes wasted in meetings that start late or overrun, time taken searching for passwords, re-scheduling conference calls, juggling slack/team/skype messages, dealing with duplicated processes as well as the core administrative tasks necessary to keep the wheels on the road.

In a perfect world, you'd do this exercise by keeping a log of your time for a fortnight or so in 15-minute chunks.

Here's a worked example. Let's say you allow 48 hours a week to work in. (Let's pretend you don't check your emails 24/7, work weekends or log on in the evenings.) Of these, 45 hours are already accounted for, so you have just three hours a week available for Head Space, or extra activities. How can you possibly pick up new responsibilities?

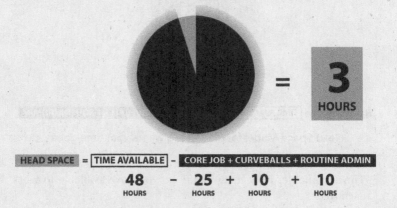

| HEAD SPACE | = | TIME AVAILABLE | − | CORE JOB + CURVEBALLS + ROUTINE ADMIN |

| 48 | − | 25 | + | 10 | + | 10 |
| HOURS | | HOURS | | HOURS | | HOURS |

Do the Head Space model on your next team offsite, to plot how well the work is distributed and who is falling victim to curveballs. You can each do your model, then plot your scores on a team version. You'll see who takes too long to get through their work and who is getting too much dumped on them because they are a victim of their own efficiency.

Your aim is to get through your tasks as efficiently as possible to create Head Space.

If you need more time for Head Space, and I reckon you do, then increasing the hours you work is _not_ the solution. You may choose to do this occasionally, and even get a kick out of it, but that should be the exception.

Being more productive isn't about doing more hours, it's about choosing tasks with the most impact. It is also about setting boundaries if the organization paying your salary assumes they are buying round the clock access to you.

The cures that follow in Part 2 will help you get on top of all this. Radical change is great, but if you aren't quite ready for a total life transformation, I suggest you pick one cure, implement it for a few weeks, then move on to the next.

PART 2

Cure

CHAPTER 3

Summary (if you don't have time to read a book)

• • •

This chapter provides a summary of the steps to getting cured for Crazy Busyness, each one freeing up incremental chunks of time. For each of the cures, there's a chapter that explores it in more detail. But if you really don't have time to read a whole book, the following is a summary of what you need to work on, so you do.

First, a reminder that how you do your job is mostly under your control. Crazy Busy people are hardwired for hard work and people-pleasing. We craft the way we work to suit these needs, but they won't make us happier or more successful.

Think about two people you work on projects with, with the same job title and objectives. One might spend long hours in front of their screen checking micro details and sending lengthy emails. The other might spend more time on the phone or face to face. They scope out project outcomes rather than heading straight for the details, they agree milestones and get stakeholder buy-in. Each person has the best of intentions, but the second is inevitably more successful and more popular too. The first is crazy busy, tired and a stress magnet.

Many of us operate somewhere in the middle. We may have learned bad habits, despite our logical mind telling us to pick up the phone and work smartly. As we've seen already, too many cultures and managers encourage Crazy Busy complexity.

These steps to curing this are all under your control, so you begin to craft your job more efficiently, regardless of the madness around you.

If some of this madness is addressed from a cultural level too then so much the better. Part 4 gives you the tools to lead others out of Crazy Busyness. Regardless of your rung on the ladder, your behaviour,

THE CRAZY BUSY CURE

success and new-found energy will rub off on your overwhelmed colleagues.

Here's a summary of what is covered in the following chapters of Part 2: Cure:

4 Start with the future you want to create and work backwards

Understand your values. Does how you spend your days reflect them? Are your goals inspiring you or getting in your way?

5 Know what your boss wants from you

It will be obvious how you should focus your time and attention when you understand the expectations you have to meet. Calculate your hourly rate and perform to that level, or even above it. You can't do everything, so stop trying. Prioritize critical tasks that move the needle. No one gets fired for just focusing on the key demands of their job description.

6 Chase antelopes, not field mice

Ruthlessly prioritize important work. Be like lions and chase antelopes, ignoring lower value, easier, field mice tasks such as emails, admin or pointless meetings. Book time in your diary to get your priority tasks done first. A timetable prevents procrastination. Schedule time around these critical tasks to fit in 'urgent' niggly small field mice too.

7 One thing at a time

Multitasking slows you down. Your brain can only concentrate on one significant task at once. When you think you are multitasking, you are actually just switching from one activity to another. You waste time trying to work out where you had got to on the original activity. Your multitasking is slowing everyone else down too. Pick your priority, complete it, then move on to the next one.

8 Get high on work

Aim for 90 minutes to two hours a day in Flow, a state of intense concentration that turbo-charges your productivity. Flow work releases intense pleasure chemicals. It is the most effective wellbeing intervention at work – and it's free. Block out Flow time with a prompt to begin it, regardless of whether you are in the mood to start or not. Your mood will catch up.

9 Meetings: much to say about nothing

Excessive meetings are one of the most common productivity hijackers. Do your actual work instead of talking about what you should be doing if you weren't in a meeting. Make an agenda and stick to it and don't let others hijack it. Prepare properly for the meetings you attend so you get the best out of them. Meetings should be for making decisions or flagging up problems. Track your meeting performance to see if that's the case.

10 Email less, talk more

We use our phones for everything except talking to people. Use email for the purpose it was intended: sharing documents, confirmation, summaries of conversations. Build real relationships by talking and listening. Problems escalate on email; they get solved by talking. Agree email etiquettes with your team to control it.

11 Corridor kidnappers and drive-by distractors

Get some boundaries and say 'no' to everyone who wants you NOW. 'No' is not a dirty word. Stop sacrificing your agenda on the temple of other peoples' inefficiency. Pre-empt interruptions by scheduling regular calls and check-ins in clusters. These should suit your schedule, so you don't stop your critical work throughout the day when people come to you. Stop last minute 'urgent' curveballs by asking in advance what's coming up and what people need from you, so you control the tasks to suit the rhythm of your priorities.

12 What Aristotle would say about cat videos

Wake up to the time you waste on your favourite apps. Learn some digital self-defence. Time your app and social media use. Willpower won't work, the algorithms are too powerful. Put your phone away when you are trying to concentrate.

13 The dopamine hit of a list

Clear brain fog by writing and sticking to to-do lists. It doesn't matter how high or low tech they are; the important thing is that you have a structure to remove procrastination and the element of choice. You'll enjoy the dopamine hit you get when you tick things off and, crucially, you'll be ticking the right things off, not the wrong things.

14 Ditch trying to be perfect

Working harder than everyone else and doing everything perfectly may have stood you in good stead in the past. You got promoted and rewarded for it so were tricked into thinking that you always had to meet your own impossibly high standards. With additional responsibilities you just can't do everything perfectly, and many of your tasks just need to get done to a good enough standard. Trying to be perfect just stresses you out and everyone else around you. Some jobs might need to be perfect, but most just need to get done. Check out who does well in your business; they spend very little time finessing details and much more time building networks.

CHAPTER 4

Start with the future you want to create and work backwards

• • •

- What do you want out of life?
- Does how you spend your time reflect that?
- What do you want your legacy to be?

How we spend our days is, of course, how we spend our lives.

Annie Dillard, *The Writing Life*

We are what we do all day. Make sure that how you spend your time in future reflects what's important to you.

This isn't touchy-feely stuff, it's vital in any productivity reboot.

I find that once my clients are clear on what they want, then what they should do all day, and what they should NOT do, truly clicks into place.

What are your values? What's most important to you?

Values are like a GPS navigation system, or big picture principle, for your work, career and life decision making. If you are clear on your values, then your priorities are clearer too.

Your values could be a principle, like integrity or sustainability, or something more specific to you like:

- I won't commute more than three days a week.
- Family life is my priority, so we'll try and have dinner together at least twice a week.
- I absolutely want to use my languages in my job.
- Although the next step up should be to take on more management responsibilities, it's more important to me stay hands-on with patients.
- I've got debts to pay off, so will compromise on other areas of my life until I've cleared them.

Identify your values
What are your top five values?

_____
_____
_____
_____
_____

Capture the images that come to mind immediately: the faces of your family, a neat spreadsheet, a lively sales meeting, the weights studio, feedback from happy clients. Often, you'll be taken right back to what you enjoyed doing when you were younger – the library, cycling on an open road, tinkering around in the lab or hanging out with your closest friends. This is your emotional brain making good choices for you.

_____
_____
_____
_____
_____
_____
_____
_____
_____

START WITH THE FUTURE YOU WANT TO CREATE AND WORK BACKWARDS

> Does how you spend your time reflect your values? Rate yourself
> on each one. You can even get others to rate you too. What do
> they think motivates you?
>
> _____
> _____
> _____
> _____
> _____
> _____
> _____
> _____
> _____

Nailing down what's really important to you – that honest answer that comes straight from the heart – will give you a clear indication of why you have to stop being Crazy Busy. If how you live your life disconnects with your values, then whatever you do won't ever feel quite right, despite the extrinsic trappings of success you may acquire. Somehow, you will always feel a bit hollow.

Are your values congruent with your behaviour?

For example, if intellectual challenge or being innovative is more important to you than managing a large team, then can you change your role to incorporate more time doing that – put your hands up for a creative/strategic side project, and step off the traditional management track for a while.

If being curious about new cultures is important to you, but you have no travel opportunities, then at least find time to properly get to know your colleagues from different cultural heritages. And can you find some international projects/clients? If it's not written down as a goal it won't happen.

If one of your values is being healthy, and you aren't blocking out time to do exercise, well... you know the rest. Or family, and so on. If you are a manager who claims to value kindness, but you haven't got time to develop your team or you talk over them in meetings, then you aren't really being kind are you?

Focus on saving wasted hours, not precious minutes with other people.

Don't try to save a few minutes here and there when interacting with others. Make the call, have the conversation, ask how they are, what are they working on and how's everything going. Social connections are the glue that build careers and networks. More importantly, they make most of us happier. Extrovert or not, invest time to get to know people.

You can save much bigger chunks of time by avoiding meaningless activities that swallow up the hours – social media, junk TV, newsfeeds, pointless meetings.

Why bother rushing around like the White Rabbit in Alice in Wonderland, only to spend hours in a rambling agenda-less meeting instead? We'd all be so much more successful if we pushed back on the hours wasted in that meeting, rather than falsely saving a few minutes talking to people to learn more about them.

Make time to listen, not tell

I was asked to coach Clara, a head of procurement who had received very negative feedback. She'd joined a pharmaceutical company in a newly created role and two teams were amalgamated under her. Keen to build early credibility, she'd focused on spending time with her multiple stakeholders, not building capability within her own unit.

Clara's 360-degree feedback exercise was a powder keg. Often people just hint at how they feel in these exercises, nervous of repercussions if they upset their manager. You have to read between the lines to get the real picture. In Clara's case, no one held back because they felt they had nothing to lose.

One person said that Clara was simply impossible to get hold of, postponing and never bothering to reschedule their one-to-ones. Consequently, this person was under-performing and didn't know how to correct it. Another said that when he did get a meeting with her, Clara kept interrupting and he got the feeling that she 'wanted to wrap it up as quickly as possible and move on, she was barely in the room'.

Clara was mortified. Her in-built yearning to please everyone meant that she hadn't pleased the people that were most important to her – her own team. There was no point in her building strategic partnerships and pushing for greater credibility for her division, if her own team thought she wasn't accessible. They didn't have a warm relationship with her at all. In her feedback, one person had used the term 'self-interested' to describe her.

It's no coincidence that Clara found it impossible to get airtime with her own manager. She had assumed that was the way things were done in the organization – let people get on with it until they hit a block. She hadn't questioned the Crazy Busy culture.

Clara's career took a giant leap when she realized what she'd done. Like all of us, we learn through failure rather than success. She could have thrown in the towel and switched to a role with less direct reports and more opportunity for her to develop her profile as procurement subject matter expert. She didn't. She wanted to grow as a leader, so focused her attention on that. She completely adjusted how she worked, taking a step back to listen and learn everything about the people who worked for her.

Change your mindset to maximize your potential.

Coaches like me fight over clients like Clara who want to learn and grow. Clients who are happy to push themselves beyond their current capability, who make mistakes along the way and learn from them.

This is called a growth mindset: the belief that our capability isn't fixed and that we will get better through persistence and effort. If something is important to us, then we will keep at it. We might struggle a bit, but we'll keep going, improving all the time and learning as we go.

Dr Carol Dweck, an award-winning professor at Stanford University, wrote a ground-breaking book on this. She explains that children with a growth mindset understand that they get smarter: intelligence can be developed. Children with a fixed mindset believe that their talents are inborn or fixed. Failure is proof of their limitation, not an opportunity to learn from their mistakes. This means that they will keep doing the same thing over and over, to reinforce their sense of competence, rather than challenging themselves with something new. They'd rather redo an easy puzzle than move onto a harder one. They think they are no good at a subject so give it up.

Dweck trained children to have a growth mindset, so they viewed themselves as capable of growing their intelligence. They worked harder and longer on tackling maths problems that they had previously given up on.

What's this got to do with productivity? If you have a fixed mindset then you will keep doing the same activities that give you the same performance rating. That's not being productive. It's being busy. It's like keeping your weights low in a spin class: you're giving the appearance of pushing yourself but you're not really.

If you come to work with a growth mindset, you'll take on the challenges that push the needle. People with a growth mindset know their real priorities and aren't frightened to tackle them. They allow themselves time to get into Flow. They don't sabotage their prospects by staying busy: classic fixed-mindset behaviour. They take the risk to attempt something daunting, the game-changing opportunities that were previously seen as unachievable in their business.

Changing to a growth mindset will make all the difference to your productivity. Otherwise you stay safe, mired in the weeds, or at least carrying out safe activities that don't reflect your hourly rate and job title.

Where can you push yourself a bit harder?

Obviously, sometimes it's unwise to go out on a limb and experiment. There are times in business when staying well within your comfort zone gives you a higher standard of performance. That's why it's called a comfort zone! But not always. Organizations get their competitive edge from creativity and innovation. They need people with a growth mindset, who are prepared to experiment, be different and take calculated risks.

Talent acquisition departments spot this gulf in mindsets all the time. The people with a growth mindset receive their call, listen to the role and say 'yes, tell me more'. The people with a fixed mindset say they don't feel quite ready for the challenge yet and could they talk again in a year's time when they have developed every skill mentioned in the role description? They aren't prepared to struggle a bit and to find the job harder than the one they are doing now, as they grow into it. They don't think about what they can do, they think about what they can't. They miss out because they want to stay safe. Ironically, staying safe usually achieves exactly the opposite. I've never seen 'doesn't take risks' on a list of desired competencies. (Leaving aside pilots, obviously!)

Are you obsessed with the wrong goals?

This book is all about ensuring that how you spend your time reflects your personal and professional goals and that you prioritize accordingly. This is the bedrock of executive coaching.

Most of us use a model like John Whitmore's GOAL framework in our sessions: Goal, Reality, Options, Will. Loosely this is: what do you want, what is your current situation, how badly do you want to change and what could get in the way of that change? Once the client identifies the 'right' goal, then everything else clicks into place.

Let's drill down a bit into goal setting though. Goals shouldn't be too rigid. If they are, we risk missing serendipitous opportunities that aren't on our road map.

A perfect illustration of how goals can backfire is economist Colin Camerer's study of New York cab drivers on rainy days. Demand for cabs surges when it rains. At the same time, the supply of cabs diminishes. That's not just because all the drivers are busy. Camerer and his colleagues discovered that the problem was that the drivers met their financial goals early when it rained and so headed home sooner. New York taxi drivers rent their vehicles in 12-hour shifts and set themselves a daily goal of making double that money. On rainy days they hit that goal early. Rather than cleaning up, they stick rigidly to their daily goal and finish work as soon as they hit it.

The drivers preferred the regularity of their daily target to the uncertainty of the possibility of earning more. A fixed mindset for sure.

Keep questioning your goals and keep them flexible.

I've noticed that my more successful clients seem comfortable to give new things a go, but stop doing them if they aren't working. They have a more flexible, courageous approach. They have goals and objectives of course; this is the real business world we are talking about. But their motivation is much more about committing wholeheartedly to what they do, doing their best and seeing how far they can go, then changing tack, if necessary, if that serves them better.

They are more tolerant of uncertainty about where they will end up, but they know what feels to be the right direction and that they are doing their best. They are motivated more by feelings and values – does it feel right to them? They aren't frightened to make a U-turn if it doesn't.

As journalist Oliver Burkeman describes it, they scramble for the next patch of firm ground, whatever direction it may be in, in the pursuit of success. Rather than being obsessed with a firm road map, they reach for that next patch of certainty then head off again in the pursuit of creating something special. They check that they are moving towards the right outcome, but they aren't fussed about the small checks and balances along the way.

To be clear, my clients are all in business, often doing invisible 'knowledge' work. They aren't fixing delicate equipment where every single thing has to be absolutely perfect. They don't have a rigid focus on a short-term goal and, instead, think about doing something even bigger and better. Why go for a small easy sale when they could risk a much bigger one? They adopt the Stoic mindset of the ancient Greeks: what's the worst that can happen here, and if it did, what would we do about it? The worse-case scenario is often one we can cope with – or talk ourselves out of.

Is your goal an own goal?

Don't let your goal take you down a cul-de-sac. We all like feedback and sometimes our focus on short-term milestones can stop us questioning the bigger picture and our overall direction of travel.

Is this really the best way to fulfil your potential and get what you want? Could you get there more quickly, easily? Don't make life harder than it is already.

_____

_____

_____

_____

_____

What help or support do you need?

_____

_____

_____

_____

_____

_____

_____

_____

_____

Choose a flexible, growth mindset: head up, looking around. Crazy Busy people have their heads down in the details and don't take time to question where they are going and why. As we've seen, this can be catastrophic.

Now you've checked in with what's important to you, let's clarify the greatest contribution you can make to others.

CHAPTER 5

Know what your boss wants from you

• • •

- How do you know if you are doing a good job?
- What's your manager's agenda and how do you contribute to it?
- Who are the main stakeholders? Who has the greatest influence?
- How did the people at the top of your organization get to where they are today? What does this tell you about the culture of the business?

Once you know exactly what your job performance is measured on, it should be much easier to prioritize and be productive.

Knowing what is required of you shouldn't be a big ask, should it?

Clarity of expectations should be obvious, but it is not always clear as organizations' expectations constantly shift. When I ask audiences if they know exactly what their performance is measured on, usually only about half the hands go up. That means 50 per cent are set up to fail.

Job description 101

I used to own a recruitment business. The most important lesson recruiters were taught was that the success of a match between candidate and company was dependent on how accurate the job description was. If there was a problem down the line and the person was derailed, it was inevitably because the job description wasn't clear enough. The new person wasn't doing what the company wanted because they hadn't explicitly told them. Mind-reading should have been on their list of competencies.

New hires often try to nail every task in their role description. This is impossible. Their area of focus should be right at the very top, in the job purpose section. If they threw the kitchen sink at this bit, it really wouldn't matter if they didn't deliver on the content of page two.

In reality, job descriptions are often cut and pasted from a previous version by HR or resourcing anyway, so are well out of date. They might include everything the company might ask you to do, so you can't sue them. The main deliverables get lost.

Even if the emphasis was made clear at interview, it can shift by the time you join. Contexts and people change constantly.

To add to the confusion, the real focus of the job can get buried deliberately. A customer service associate's bonus might come solely from up-selling products but that's a bit off-brand, so they don't tell people how hard they are expected to sell. There can be an expectation for new managers to make tough team changes quickly, but that's a tricky conversation to have explicitly.

It is not uncommon to report to several different bosses, with conflicting agendas. Who has the most influence on your career?

There's lots of potential for ambiguity. Ask detailed questions to ensure expectations are absolutely transparent. Repeat the conversation every six months or so if you feel you need more clarity.

Ask questions like:

- Out of everything I do, what's most important?
- How do I know I am doing a good job?
- What's the gap I need to cover in order to reach the next promotion grade?
- If you were me, what would you prioritize?
- I have taken on lots of extra projects, where should I focus for the next six months?
- If, in a year's time, you think I'm the best hire you've made, what will I have achieved?

And ask yourself this one:

- If I look back in two years and everything has gone wrong, what did I fail to do?

Once you've clarified what you are measured on then you know what needs to be prioritized.

The next stage is to ensure you choose work that adds the most value. You can start eliminating low value tasks and curveballs that don't reflect your core strengths or goals.

Where can you add the most value?

I'm a fan of Tim Ferriss' work. I hand out copies of *The 4-Hour Work-week* all the time to my clients, to help them drill down into where they can add most value, and then focus their time around doing just that.

If they aren't adding maximum value, what are they doing with their time instead?

Reading that book made me start to rethink my Crazy Busy approach to my career and life. I didn't want to become the unfulfilled busy person his book is aimed at and I didn't want to slog along until I retired to have the life I want. Of course, we can't have a four-hour work week, I doubt that Ferriss himself does. He has been criticized for tapping into the emptiness of middle-income screen-bound workers looking for a dream. What's wrong with a dream? We can all learn from his chutzpah in questioning how we spend our time.

Here are two great principles from the book:

- Just because something takes a long time doesn't make it important.

- Spending a lot of time on something doesn't make it important either.

Both so obvious, but we are all guilty of these fundamental errors. Humans love that security blanket of busyness.

Organizational life often encourages this competitive, 'I'm busier than you' attitude. I was asked to coach a Crazy Busy CEO because she said to a stressed, overwhelmed team member: 'We're all busy here, suck it up.' No guesses why she couldn't keep hold of anyone. (If people make this kind of comment to you, then make sure you read the chapter on Crazy Busy bullies.)

If your earlier career involved billable hours – accounting for every minute – it's hard to lift out of that and think the opposite: 'What's the quickest way and best way of getting this done?' or 'How can we shave off time next time?' It feels wrong to create free time. Well that's old school. I want a life, thank you, and to be defined by more than just my work.

- What do you want to be known for?
- What would an outstanding performer in your role aim for?

I work for myself and am fortunate to love what I do. Tim Ferriss is a wealthy tech entrepreneur and investor. I realize that you may not have the luxury of picking and choosing the tasks you do so you might be feeling annoyed here or disempowered. Hang on.

My job as a coach is to point out blind spots to make my clients more aware of how they think and behave. Then to encourage their belief that they can do something about the elements they can control. What CAN you control about your workload?

You can ask the person who gives you a report to write every week which parts they find most interesting and how you can make it more concise 'for them'. You can say no to helping organize a client function because, ultimately, no one really appreciates the heroes behind the scenes do they? They value the ones out front, charming the clients.

There's plenty more practical advice in the remaining chapters as to how you can do your work more efficiently by choosing the most impactful tasks.

What's your game-changer?

Usually there is one significant priority which would have an over-arching effect on your career, I call it your game-changer. If we got it done it would make such a difference that we might not even need to tackle your other priorities. Which one is it? How much time do you honestly spend on it now?

When I ask my clients how much time they spend on their real game-changer they often say, 'Oh that one, yes zero per cent, maybe five if I'm lucky.'

Find your game-changer

If you knew that whatever you focused on next would succeed, what would you aim for?

_____

_____

_____

_____

_____

That's your Game-changer.
What would achieving it mean to you?

_____

_____

_____

_____

What's got to go to make space for it?

_____

_____

_____

_____

_____

My favourite way to prioritize is next up.

CHAPTER 6

Chase antelopes, not field mice

• • •

- Do you spend all day chasing small stuff?
- Do you get a kick from ticking things off lists?
- Do you worry about what you haven't done, rather than being pleased with what you have done?

Human beings are hard-wired to be busy, the rest of the animal kingdom not so much. My dog has her dinner and a walk then is happy to nap. She doesn't walk the boundaries of our house, sniffing every corner, just to give herself something to do. We humans, on the other hand, love the dopamine hit of being busy – crossing anything off a list feels good. Consequently, we fill our lists and days with small crazy busy stuff that really doesn't move us forward. Most of us are driven by all the small stuff in our inbox, which turns itself into our daily to-do list.

The antelope/field mice analogy isn't mine, but I love it. Lions don't bother to chase field mice or whatever cute little critters they see around them. The effort required to spot one, leap up, chase it, kill it, digest it, share it with the pride, just wouldn't be worth the calorific intake. They'd die out. Instead, they spend their days just chasing antelopes that they can get a big meal out of. In between antelopes, they chill out and recover.

Do you spend your time on antelopes – those priority tasks, the game-changers – or lots of little, safe field mice that keep you busy and distracted but add little value? That is the essence of Crazy Busyness.

Unlike the lions, we can schedule our antelopes, especially when we need to block out large chunks of time.

Plan a week in advance if you can. Or ask yourself every morning: 'What do I absolutely need to get done today?' We used to aim for three things, I think a single critical one is enough and if you get more done, that's a bonus. Be kind to yourself and have realistic expectations.

We can over-estimate how long it takes to get small things done (that difficult but crucial conversation may just take two minutes) and, equally, under-estimate how long it takes to create something from scratch.

Here's my process for scheduling and achieving your priority tasks. It eliminates the opportunity to procrastinate.

Identify a priority task/antelope and ring-fence the time you are going to do it.

PIMP process for achieving priority tasks

Priority: What's the one thing you must get done? Estimate how much time it will take. If you haven't done the task before, can you ask someone who has so you can get a reasonable estimate? Most people don't track how long it takes to complete all their job functions. Remember Parkinson's Law? Work expands to fill the time available. If we allow too much time we faff around and procrastinate then do it at the last minute. If we underestimate the time instead, we risk missing deadlines and stressing out people who are waiting downstream. Time tracking gets you back in control of your job role.

Insert: Stick the task in your calendar. Get into the habit of budgeting your time to your tasks like this, rather than fitting your priorities around the sides of all the routine work you do. Calendars should be full of tasks not meetings! Block out a slot in your calendar and also the new location if you need to move to get it done without distraction. Check in with the people most likely to sling curveballs at you ('can you just...') to see if they need anything from you and maybe arrange to check in again with them after your time slot. It's your choice if you tell them when you won't be available and why. You can disappear for an hour or two without the sky falling in.

Mean: Commit to doing the task. Nailing your priorities is career-enhancing and a massive boost to your wellbeing. Push back on the hijackers who want you to do something else for them instead. You might also feel a bit mean too, because (ridiculously) it feels selfish to put your own work ahead of pleasing everyone else. If people need you urgently during that time then that's invariably down to their disorganization and their expectation (set by you) that you will drop everything to help them. Train them to work in a more organized, planned way. This can be done diplomatically. *'I've noticed that quite often you ask me for data at short notice, maybe we could check in quickly every morning to see what you've got coming up, so I can take more time to prepare properly for you.'*

Prompt: Fix a trigger to start PIMP time. This is the habit that makes all the difference. Discipline yourself to have a clear point to stop what you are working on, bang on time, and switch automatically to the priority task. The prompt could be an alarm, or after an event, like straight after a meeting. There will always be small stuff to do; plan to do it when you finish your PIMP time. Do not get distracted by emails or chat, stick to the plan. This is where good PAs come in. Move from your desk if you can, or at least shut down notifications, hide your phone and start.

Try this process for a week and see the difference it makes to output and how good you feel.

If you can, aim for one slot of 90/120 minutes PIMP time a day, ideally in 'Flow' (more on this in Chapter 8). That is the holy grail of productivity.

How to go after your biggest game-changers/ antelopes

Sometimes we have to go after really substantial antelopes. I've helped clients with funding applications, pitches, curveball projects – all sorts of priorities that have meant they've had to drop everything and focus on one thing.

Clear your schedule. Allocate a large chunk of time (even a week or more) and sprint through it all at once, rather than trying to do it in fragments. If it's important, give yourself every chance of doing it to the very best of your ability. And don't even think about getting it done at the place you normally work – you'll just get distracted and interrupted.

Allow figuring-out time. You put off this task because you have no idea how to go about it. Don't put yourself under pressure to start it. The first block of time should be allocated to figuring it out HOW to start it. What resources do you need, who has done it before, where can you work without interruption, what end result do you want and so on. We all know that every project goes wrong if the scoping phase is rushed, so that needs to be properly scheduled in too.

WHY YOU NEED TO PIMP YOUR FIELD MICE TOO

Psychologists have identified something called the Zeigarnik effect – the tendency of the human mind to fixate on unfinished or interrupted tasks rather than completed ones. Russian psychologist Bluma Zeigarnik studied the phenomenon after discovering that waiters had better recollection of unpaid bills than paid ones. In Crazy Busyness, rather than feeling proud of the antelopes we've laid to rest, we stress about all the field-mice we still have to tackle.

The solution to this source of stress is identified by psychologist Derek Draper in his book *Create Space*. We don't need to *do* the small stuff. We just need to make a plan for *when* we will do them. PIMPing time to do the small stuff reassures us that we'll get them done. We can maintain our attention on the less urgent but more important task in front of us now, and focus.

DOES RUTHLESSLY PRIORITIZING MAKE YOU FEEL GUILTY?

You know what you are measured on, you've done the Head Space exercise, but you still have too much on your plate. Here's an exercise to help the penny drop.

What's your hourly rate?

Work out what you earn per hour, or what your company bills you out at, if appropriate. How much of your time justifies that amount?

_____

_____

_____

_____

_____

_____

_____

_____

_____

NOW WHAT NEEDS TO GO?

Being assertive is easier said than done. Managers know they should delegate more but I often catch my clients mired in non-critical activities. This means they don't have time to train and develop their teams, particularly the B players who aren't pulling their weight. Consequently, the workflow is unevenly distributed and performance slips, giving managers an even bigger excuse to get back in the detail.

It's not easy to resist the siren song of work that's below your pay grade. It remains our comfort zone – we are good at it which is why we got promoted. We get promoted so we stop doing it!

Here's the one question that gets to the heart of it:

What is it that only you can do?

Make a list of everything else you do now and ponder these questions:

- Who needs coaching or training to develop their skills so you can give them more to do?

  _____

  _____

- Who can you outsource to, delegate to, hand it back to?

  _____

  _____

- Who are your lowest performing team members who don't pull their weight and what's your plan to develop or exit them?

  _____

  _____

- Who is coasting at the top of their comfort zone and capable of taking on even more?

  _____

  _____

- Who are you covering for or mopping up after and why do you do that? Managers nip problems in the bud, not cover them up. You might want to read up on co-dependency, there's a reference to a great book in the list at the end. Many of us have had to work on this.

  _____

  _____

  _____

  _____

- Do you need additional support or resources to achieve your objectives and how will you make the business case to get them? When will you start writing your proposal?

  _____

  _____

  _____

  _____

- If you spend far too much time on routine admin, could you justify hiring a fierce PA to manage your diary, patrol your boundaries and pick up everything that's below your pay-grade? A good one is infinitely worth the investment.

_____

_____

You can only chase one antelope at a time. I'll explain why in the next chapter.

CHAPTER 7

One thing at a time

• • •

- Ever shut down your computer and found emails that you thought you'd sent, but hadn't actually finished writing?
- How many screens are you looking at when you work? One, two, plus your phone, TV, more?

You cannot focus on more than one task at a time. No one can. But some of us are in the habit of bombarding our brains with data, constantly multitasking across digital channels. Ofcom claim that 27 per cent of 18–34-year-olds engage in at least five online activities while commuting, compared to only 9 per cent of over-35s.

Does this habit mean you can concentrate on more than one thing at once when you get to the office? No! I don't care what gender or generation you are.

Research by Eyal Ophir, Clifford Nass, and Anthony D Wagner tells us that heavy multitaskers are less mentally organized and have a hard time differentiating relevant from irrelevant details.

Here's an example of heavy multitasking: you are on a conference call, reading your emails at the same time, over-hearing chat across the desk, wondering why your other colleague isn't speaking up on that call, worrying about a difficult conversation you have to have after lunch, you feel hungry, which reminds you that you need to go home via the supermarket, that reminds you that your child didn't take their coat to school and it might rain, there's a slack message, plus another email has arrived and there are cheers at the tennis match on the screen behind you (for 'staff wellbeing') with a news ticker displayed on it.

It doesn't matter how smart you are, a genius or a goldfish, your brain is full. No wonder we feel overwhelmed. Psychologist George A. Miller tells us that our short-term memories can only process about seven pieces of information at once and that we can only concentrate on one significant, cognitive, task at once.

We can do an easy physical task, or one we are good at, and a mental task at the same time. Going for a walk to think about a problem for example, or ironing while watching TV.

Background noise is fine for some of us. You can complete routine tasks like clearing your emails with music on. You can't draft a document when you are trying to pay attention to a podcast. You can pay attention in a meeting or you can read your emails. Not both. You can listen, or you can write, or you can read. Not all at once.

Multitasking is a misnomer.

When we think we are multitasking we are actually just switching from one task to another.

Switching costs are the cost of lost time when we mentally transition from one task to another and have to reorient back on to the original topic. Recent estimates in the *Journal of Experimental Psychology* suggest that we can lose up to 40 per cent of our productivity this way.

Here are the facts:

- It takes longer to achieve tasks if you switch between them rather than if you complete one and then move onto the next one.

- You make more mistakes when you switch than if you do one job at a time.

- The more complex the task, the more mistakes you'll make if you switch.

- Once you are distracted it can take much longer than the length of the distraction to re-start the task. If the task is complicated you may not even go back to it, because you don't have time to catch up on where you were.

This is why it is so important to block out time in the PIMP process to nail your priority tasks – those antelopes. You are giving yourself the luxury of doing one thing at once. You'll do it better and quicker and enjoy the dopamine hit of getting something done. It's much less stressful.

Multitasking slows everyone else down too.

One of the major causes of project failure is people multitasking rather than making concerted progress on their priority task.

If you have three tasks to do, and do a bit of each one, then you might feel great because you are making progress on each one. By the end of the first day you've done a third of each one.

On the second day, you've done another third of each one – nearly there, you're winning. On day three, you've done all of them.

That's all fine unless, downstream, someone is waiting for you to complete the first task so they can get on with their work. They won't receive it until the end of day three.

If they follow your example and multi-task as well, then it has a domino effect on the entire workflow, delaying the whole project.

One thing at a time!

CHAPTER 8

Get high on work

• • •

- When were you last completely absorbed in a task?
- How often do you feel that sense of extreme satisfaction from really using your head and completing something significant?
- Why is it so hard to work like this every day?

When you are working on your priorities in the PIMP process, you should be able to get into a state of optimal concentration called 'Flow'. All the evidence tells us that this state of peak performance is the secret to success and happiness at work. When we are deeply concentrating, lost in our work, we feel our best and perform our best.

In a ten-year study conducted by McKinsey, executives reported that they were five times more productive when they consistently worked in a Flow state for a day a week. As author Steven Kotler points out, that means they could get as much done by the end of Monday than their steady-state peers did in a whole week.

Is a full day in Flow a leap too far? It certainly is for me: a half day is more than enough. The same McKinsey researchers said that if we could all just increase the time we spend in Flow by 15–20 per cent, overall workplace productivity would almost double. Think about the difference that would make!

And really, how difficult should this be? To concentrate for up to two hours a day? We are twenty-first century knowledge workers and have created working environments that make concentrating a rare occurrence!

What is Flow and how do we achieve it?

The mental state of Flow was named by Hungarian psychologist Mihaly Csikszentmihalyi to describe the feeling of total immersion or concentration in a task. It's when you are lost in what you do, ignoring all distractions and feeling totally focused and energized. Csikszentmihalyi was fascinated by how some artists became absorbed in their work. They lost their sense of time, appetite, even a sense of their own ego. He researched these optimal experiences and called this state 'Flow', using the metaphor of water carrying people along.

To observe Flow, watch top sports people intensely concentrating, when nothing else matters to them. Flow has been described as blissful: our emotions are channelled into performing a task and we are positively absorbed in thinking and learning.

People who successfully master the Flow state report powerful personal breakthroughs including earning more, working less hours and feeling aligned with their life purpose.

People who don't find Flow may experience work as merely a necessary evil. Roman Krznaric, at the School of Life, says that Flow is one of three vital components for work to be truly fulfilling. The others are freedom (over your time and labour) and meaning – finding value in what you do.

So how can we tap into this joy? How should you set up the right conditions for your staff to both enjoy their work and perform at their peak through Flow?

Flow feels great!

Really great actually! Hyper-concentrating like this releases the pleasure chemicals dopamine, serotonin, endorphins, oxytocin, norepinephrine and anandamide. You are getting all these legal highs all at once from WORK.

What a great manager you would be if you could get your team bonding over these intense pleasures that come from deep working.

You aren't handing out psychedelic drugs – you are merely creating the conditions that allow them to get right in their heads and do their best work. Not only would they be happier, they'd be more productive and successful too. And work fewer hours.

Tips for getting in and staying in Flow

- Above all, it won't happen unless you plan it. That's your new mantra: if it's not scheduled it won't get done. Follow the PIMP process to make it happen.
- Get your environment right – move location if you need to. I rarely meet anyone who can get real Flow working done at their desk, even with headphones on. Even when working remotely you might find it harder to concentrate on something meaningful in the same place you toggle between routine tasks. I get most of my Flow working done in coffee shops – even noisy ones. I go with the intention of writing something and just get on with it. There must be quiet places in your office you can move to.
- Kill potential distractions and interruptions – block the time out in your calendar and switch off your chat, social media, email and all channels. Tell people that you are going to concentrate on something for a couple of hours, allocate time before the PIMP time to make sure they have everything you need from you and tell them when you will be available again. If there's a genuine important or urgent situation, they'll find you.
- Common sense dictates that there will be better times of the week to do it than others. It's unlikely you'll get away without interruption at 10 am on a Monday, but Friday afternoons are a great time. Start with once a week and build up to making two hours a day part of your routine and, better still, everyone in your team's routine.
- Don't expect Flow to hit straight away. Studies show that it can take between five to twenty minutes to kick in. Increase your tolerance levels to put up with the frustration of getting going. Schedule a time to start – using PIMP – and well, start!
- Remove the unhelpful emotions that get in the way also. Achieving flow involves a realistic perception of your skillset. You will cloud this perception with thoughts like 'I can't do this, it will be rubbish, someone else could do this better, what's the point anyway, etc.'. You could of course be right, but these limiting assumptions stop you from giving it your best shot or asking for support when you need help.

- Know where you are on the task. Csikszentmihalyi says you stay focused and engaged by the constant awareness of what is next. Make a plan and tick off where you have got up to.
- Take short breaks and make sure you aren't dehydrated. Train yourself to drop back into the Flow state quickly when you start work again and steer clear of other tasks that could interrupt your concentration. I can't do more than 90 minutes without a quick break, but it doesn't take me long to restart if I am on a sprint.
- Finally, in the unlikely event that my children are reading this, getting lost on social media isn't Flow because there is no challenge and you aren't learning. The intense concentration that comes from gaming isn't Flow either – it is hyper-focus, which leaves you in a wound-up, aggressive state, not a happy Flow one. Too much time in either of these zones makes it harder to shift to the optimal concentration you need to be super effective.

ECSTASY AT WORK: TEAM FLOW EXPERIENCES

Extraordinarily intense Flow states are called *ecstasis*. This comes from ancient Greek and means 'a moment when you stand outside your ordinary self and feel connected to something much greater than you'. It's an out of the ordinary state of consciousness. In the classical and Christian worlds, this ecstasy (derived from *ecstasis*) usually involved a trance-like connection to a god or spirit. Philosopher Jules Evans has written about the influence of these profound experiences. He tells us how Plato identified that artists were unusually susceptible to ecstasy or divine mania. They literally breathed in the spirit and created great works without entirely knowing how they did (Jules Evans, *The Art of Losing Control: A Philosopher's Search for Ecstatic Experience*).

Today scientists, Silicon Valley executives and special operators like Navy SEALs and Green Berets are gaining insights into how individuals and teams can harness these profound Flow states and use them to escalate performance. Their goal is the competitive edge that comes with deeper collective thinking, for example, when instant responses or deeply creative solutions are required. Synching your brains together, as in a hive mind, can shift consciousness to get to these ideas quicker and better.

CAN WE ALL GET INTO THE ZONE?

I suspect that shutting off the senses with group mystical experiences might be too much of a leap in your organization. You can still send productivity and wellbeing through the roof by trialling some group Flow sessions. These used to be simply called everyone 'working' or 'concentrating' back in the day, so really there shouldn't need to be so much of a drama about them.

Can you synchronize the times where people get on with their deep Flow working together, without interrupting each other? To be clear, this is not 90/120 minutes of doing your admin. It's space to start a challenging piece of work (antelope, priority, you get it) that involves some real deep concentrating. You may get push back on that because people aren't used to doing it. They even feel guilty about it. How nice it is to use their brains for once, they probably haven't really felt that way since they did their finals.

You'll have to start ten minutes or so before with a reminder: 'Have you all got everything you need before we start, so we don't interrupt each other?' You may need to have one team member to man the phones or team email address. You might have to make a point of all showing that you are unavailable on your calendars and communication channels. You definitely need to hide all phones.

Ideally, you'd do this at a set (PIMP) time daily for up to two hours. If every day is too much of a stretch, how about Flow Friday afternoons to start with?

I'd try them in the early afternoon when you aren't too tired but not so hyper-alert that your brain wants to toggle between different channels as usual. I find I am more creative when I am a bit tired, and my brain isn't so good at filtering out my less logical ideas.

The benefit of all doing this together is, of course, that you get to do deep working at your desk. In addition, there'd be a group sense of shared satisfaction at actually all using their heads together, even if you aren't totally getting out of them.

Most people struggle to find Flow time until they push back on their meeting commitments to create some space in their diaries.

CHAPTER 9

Meetings

Much to say about nothing

• • •

- Do you track how effective your meetings are?
- Do your meetings have a clear purpose?
- Who doesn't get heard in meetings you attend and why not?

Well-run meetings and one-to-ones are crucial touch points for building trust in your team and getting stuff done. Badly run meetings are an incredibly expensive use of resource. It is a mystery to me why organizations don't get a grip on this.

Training your staff to run meetings effectively is one of the best investments you will make. It's a cultural change that shows you respect your own time and other people's.

The true cost of meetings

Here's an example of a fairly typical situation. There are ten full-time team members. Each person attends four internal meetings a week, booked into the diary for an hour each, because Outlook does that automatically. They usually start at least five minutes late because some people rush straight from another meeting. One meeting regularly over-runs by twenty minutes and another one, a project update, could be replaced with a snappy two-minute video.

Add on top the wasted time when they come out of the meeting. Ofcom say we check our phone every 12 minutes. Who doesn't check their messages when they leave the meeting room? We grab a coffee, have a chat, look at our inbox, check WhatsApp, get lost in a newsfeed.

People report that it takes up to twenty-five minutes to get back into the zone (measure it yourself to see).

That's over 200 minutes wasted per person per week and over 33 hours a week wasted across the entire team.

That's the equivalent of having one team member work on Mondays only, then take the rest of the week off. From Tuesdays to Fridays headcount is down to nine, not ten, just because of inefficient meetings.

AGENDA-LESS STREAMS OF CONSCIOUSNESS

Often relatively junior people invite us to meetings. We feel it is impolite to turn down the request, then turn up to an agenda-less free for all, without the information we need because we've no time or information to prepare.

There's rarely a consequence if someone hasn't completed the action they said they would. We go off topic and, too often, empty vessels make the most noise. The real decisions get made afterwards, in the meeting about the meeting, often upsetting some egos in the process.

Learn how to chair meetings and then teach others how to do it properly: to manage distractions, set the context, keep to the agenda, state the objectives, encourage collaboration, manage difficult personalities and encourage opinions from the people closest to the problem – who often have the best solutions, but may feel intimidated to share their opinion.

Meeting protocols to put in place from now on

More than three in a meeting or conference call? Don't attend if there isn't an agenda. Otherwise you need another meeting to provide the information that came up in the discussion. If you are invited to a meeting without an agenda say 'sorry, I just don't have capacity for that, but please email me the action points after the meeting'. Explain that you need to prepare all the information required so a decision can be made. That's the purpose of a meeting: to make decisions. If it is all FYI stuff, then share the information in a different way, a quick video is way more effective.

No agenda, no meeting.

My favourite agenda structure is the 3Ps. I've come across various iterations of this, here's mine:

- **Purpose:** Why are we holding the meeting? If you ask this as a question, you are more likely to get the exact answer you want. *'What's the budget and predicted profit margin for proposed Chesham office?'*

- **Process:** State the contribution you require from each person at the meeting in order to achieve that purpose. This means that people who aren't named in a contribution don't need to make one, apart from participating in the decision. It also means no horrible surprises when you are asked a question that you haven't prepared for. Equally, if you are named in the process and don't prepare your contribution, then the spotlight is on your poor performance.

- **Pay-off:** Specifically what you want to leave the room with. *'After hearing all the contributions, we will decide whether or not to go ahead with the Chesham office and agree the scoping process and timescales.'*

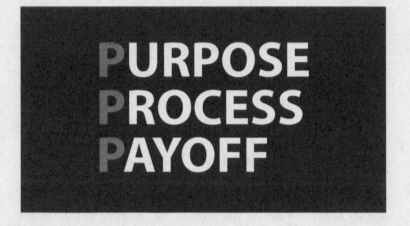

If a structure seems like a leap too far then try a question to haul everyone back to the main point or cut through all the conversations.

I have a 'Rule of Just One Thing' when I am coaching, which you can use in meetings too. Out of everything, what's the one problem/decision/issue we should deal with:

- Given all of this, what's most important for us to deal with right now?

- What's the greatest challenge we are facing?
- What's the real issue here?

More meeting tactics

Here's more ways my clients have cut back on meeting time:

- Can you change your default meeting time from 60 minutes to 45? One of my clients has to book meeting rooms in hourly slots but has each meeting starting promptly at quarter past the hour, to give everyone a chance to get in the room.
- Get your facilities manager to make the lights go off after 45 minutes.
- If you take over the chairing of a meeting that seems to have too many attendees, perhaps when you join a business, go around the room at the beginning and ask them to say why they are there. If there is no reason for them to be there, or they don't know how they can contribute, then release them. They'll be forever grateful to you.
- Why invite so many people to your meetings? Decision making reduces when more than seven people get involved. One representative from each team should be enough.
- Ditch meeting FOMO. Make it part of the culture for it to be perfectly acceptable to decline meetings. Don't go in the meeting room yourself unless you are clear on why you are there and what you want to get out of it. People tell me their boss has suggested they go to a meeting, but when they get there they find it is a complete waste of time. Just say 'I've checked it out but it doesn't fit with my priorities'. Why waste huge chunks of time like this?
- Start on time. Never, ever, re-read the papers if people are expected to have studied them in advance. One option is to schedule time at the start of each meeting for people to study the information before the discussion, telling them in advance what the decision is they need to make so they can prepare accordingly.
- If it's someone else's meeting and they are off topic, get back on track by asking, 'What are we trying to achieve here?' or 'Can we just take a step back please and look again at X?'.

- Be choosy about the food and ambiance. You are setting the context for professional decision making, not a photo for Instagram. I've spotted a link in some boardrooms between waffle and carbs. Entertainment is fine if you are bringing in clients. For internal meetings you should aim to get people out of the room as fast as possible and back to doing satisfying work, on schedule. That's much better for their wellbeing than some chocolate biscuits.

- If someone senior is hijacking the time, shut them up politely: 'Those are some great points Stan, we'll come back to them on a future agenda when we have time to do them justice.' If you can, have a discrete word with them afterwards. If they want to share their knowledge, can they mentor or run a training session for some of your team?

- Put the most important item at the top of the agenda so adequate time is allowed. Avoid that archaic 'any other business' as it's a potential opportunity for people to raise new issues when you should be finishing up. If it's worthy of a mention they should get it on the agenda.

- Instead of one person taking note of all the agreed actions, and reading them out at the end, go round the room and ask people to state what they have agreed to do. Saying them out loud helps them to take ownership of their actions themselves.

- I've written at length already about how our cognitive ability declines with distractions. I'd have a rule about no phones and laptops, only for notetaking.

- If people must use PowerPoint, get them to limit it to just a few slides with only a couple of points on each one. Death by deck is way too common. Train them on how to succinctly state the key points they want people to know. Could one key point be enough? Train them on how to do presentations – it's a crucial career skill but people seem to think it should just come naturally and wing it.

Rename it

Call the meeting something compelling. Sheryl, a sales director, had a 'Thursday catch-up' as an opportunity for people to discuss how they were going to hit their weekly target with just 24 hours to go. Feedback was that many in her team dreaded it, especially if they were shy of their numbers that week. Not only did they think the meeting was pointless (they knew where they were going wrong), it made them feel worse about themselves, so they didn't feel capable of turning things around.

The obvious solution was to ditch the meeting, but the obvious solution is often the wrong one. Instead, Sheryl renamed it to 'Get out of Jail'. This drew attention to the focus of the meeting – and their role purpose – but in a light-hearted 'we are all in this together' way. She also made it 45 minutes, not in excess of an hour as before. More people turned up (they stopped making excuses not to be there) and, as energy, teamwork and morale lifted, bingo, so did sales.

Make a decision

Meetings should be for decisions and not for sharing information. Track how productive your meetings really are. Do you get decisions made and move the work along?

If you are responsible for the decision, you might need to make a tough, even unpopular call at the end of the meeting, once you have gathered all the information you need.

Start by going around the room a few times and make sure you get everyone's opinion. Aim for consensus if you can. If you don't get it, then make the decision yourself and move on. Sometimes a wrong decision is better than no decision.

> 'Thank you everyone, I've heard everyone's opinions now and appreciate all your views on this. From what I've heard, a Chesham office doesn't meet our benchmarks to justify the money the investment involved, so I am going to withdraw the plans. I'd like to look next month at how we can incorporate some of your ideas into our Head Office initiatives and will formulate an agenda to reflect these for the next meeting.'

You might want to set up a meeting etiquette, including rules like no phones, look at the person speaking, everyone gets a turn to speak for five minutes (or appropriate) without interruption, we start and finish on time, always use the 3Ps, complete actions if we agree to them.

Virtual meetings: How outstanding performers influence on Zoom

Influencing others is hard at the best of times, never mind when you aren't in the same room. Here's how to get decisions made virtually.

1. **You can't wing it anymore.** Virtual meetings are much less forgiving: waffling doesn't work so your messages have to be clearer. Take far more time to prepare. Write your points down, especially your opening pitch, and practice them out loud. Record yourself on your phone. Keep practising until you sound convincing and authoritative. Block out half an hour in your calendar before each meeting to give yourself space to do this properly. Do you ever do this, honestly?

2. **Limit your meeting attendance.** See above. Giving yourself time to get it right means that you have to cut back on less important meetings so that you can fully prepare for the significant ones.

3. **Give positive cues.** Give non-verbal cues to the person speaking in meetings to show that you support them. I do lots of virtual sessions and it is enormously reassuring when people smile and nod. Take a quick video of yourself on your phone to see what you look like just staring at the screen, then see how much friendlier you look when you smile and are animated: body language still matters.

4. **Take yourself seriously.** If you are supposed to be an expert, people expect clear logic and recommendations. Say: 'Given everything we know at the moment, my advice is...'. Use a louder voice than usual.

5. **Show up on camera.** Dial in on time, look sharp. Don't expect to have any influence if you don't turn your camera on. Visibility is credibility. Use a pre-loaded background if you prefer (if you are working from home and want to keep your space private).

6. **Work tech like a pro.** Look at the camera, not the screen, i.e. the light on the top of the screen, not the screen itself. If you talk to the camera it appears that you are looking straight in the other person's eyes. Frame yourself properly. Position your laptop so your face is straight at it: one or two cookbooks do this job perfectly. Light needs to be in front of your screen, not behind, and natural light is best. If your window is in the wrong place buy a ring light, they aren't expensive.

Meetings are the reason most people tell me they can't get their work done. It's time to move onto another problem – emails.

CHAPTER 10

Email less, talk more

● ● ●

- Is email choking the life out of you?
- Is your inbox your to-do list?
- Do you ever use your phone for phoning people?

The way we use email chokes our productivity. Email has become an invasive intrusion, binding us to our screens: the Japanese Knotweed of work. Researchers at McKinsey say we spend about 28 per cent of our time actively managing email: that's over a quarter of every day.

For most of us emailing is not our job. It's just supposed to be a tool to help us fulfil our job, but instead it interrupts us and slows us down.

Why are we so hardwired to respond straight away to messages?

Our monkey brains instinctively respond to the ping of a notification. This is partly driven by a brain phenomenon called the Urgency Effect (Zhu and Yang, 2018). Our minds prioritize immediate satisfaction (clearing emails) over long-term rewards (getting on with our antelopes).

We far prefer urgent smaller tasks with a deadline than more important tasks without an immediate time restraint. Our brain gets rewarded by the immediate and certain payoff. We even do quick tasks without a deadline because our brain fools us that we are getting stuff done.

That's why, when we don't know how to start a challenging task, or something different or more cerebral than our usual problems, we end up defaulting to checking our inbox. It's the easiest option in the short-term but we are just kidding ourselves.

TRY TO IGNORE THE PRESSURE TO RESPOND

We are always-on. We see an email and feel pressure to respond immediately, even though most messages can be dealt with later. The pressure is even more acute when working from home. We reply to emails straight away to prove we are working, when we should be off-grid and recharging our batteries or getting on with something impactful.

We shouldn't have to be always available to prove we are thinking about our work.

How to break the habit

Some people resort to one of two strategies to cope with their email:

1. They strive for inbox zero, compulsively triaging emails into folders and colour-coded systems.
2. They give up deleting and claim that, despite having 3000+ emails in their inbox, they can find what they need using keywords.

There's a middle ground:

Check your emails less. Instead of checking every thirty minutes or so, and keeping an eye on notifications in the meantime, switch off notifications and extend the time between each check. Focus on your actual work instead, scheduling time during the day to check your mail rather than being constantly aware of what's in your inbox. If you switched to hourly checking, that could cut about eight checks from your day. If each check takes about 15 minutes, you've just saved yourself two hours... You're welcome.

Move them as soon as you read them. Read them, delete them, or archive them to act on later.

Call people. We use phones for everything now except phone calls. When your email chain gets beyond two messages, pick up the phone. Get people comfortable with calling you by calling them first: that's how you build trust. That's especially true now when some of us feel disconnected and appreciate a call even more.

Agree an email etiquette to stop the problem at source. Put internal email use at the top of the agenda for your next team meeting. I promise everyone feels the same as you and will be delighted to discuss it:

- Clarify how often you check your inbox and how you want people to contact you in between if they need you.

- Agree reasonable response times to non-urgent messages.

- Decide who should be copied in on emails – obviously as few people as possible.

- Agree turns to manage @team email addresses so you don't duplicate effort.

- Decide a policy on out of hours/time-zone messages that respect your boundaries.

- Stop the back and forward thank you/acknowledgement messages.

- Provide training on how to draft punchy emails.

- Clarify in the subject line if messages require action or are for information only.

- Ask people to stop firing off emails on the hoof. If their excuse is that they don't want to forget what's on their mind, then suggest they use the Notes function instead.

- Request that people who email in the evenings send their messages to draft/themselves instead. They can forward them to you the next day once they've double-checked the tone and content. It will take just a few minutes but will avoid causing possible offence or misunderstandings. The email sent in the morning always differs from the one drafted over a glass of wine the night before.

- Call out the culprits who send two or three messages on the same topic, rather than taking time to compose one thoughtful message, or better still, call you.

- Explain your email ground rules to new starters in your team; they'll be delighted that you respect their time.

Now you've dealt with your emails, the next cure is to stop the people that interrupt you.

CHAPTER 11

Corridor kidnappers and drive-by distractors

● ● ●

- How often does someone interrupt you, saying 'can you just...?'
- How long does it take you to get back on track?
- Can you push back and let people know when you are interruptible and when you're not?

'That woman speaks eighteen languages and can't say 'No' in any of them.'

Dorothy Parker

How familiar is this scenario? You have finally got down to getting some real work done. You've followed the PIMP process: scheduled it, started it and are getting absorbed in it. You've switched off notifications or turned your phone off. It feels great.

So far, so good.

Then along comes one of your colleagues, oblivious to your blissful state of Flow: 'Hey, have you got a minute, I just want to run something past you?'

Some interruptions are welcome. You might catch mistakes early, so work doesn't have to be redone later. The trick is to make sure it's done on your terms, clustered into a time-slot that suits you. These time bandits, corridor kidnappers, drive-by distractors – whatever you want to call them – need to be managed tactfully.

Let's get some data for why frequent interruptions are a problem.

Author Peter Bregman quotes a study conducted by Microsoft Corporation on interruptions. They taped 29 hours of people working and found that, on average, they were interrupted four times per hour. (That seems quite low, compared to many of the people I talk to about this.)

Here's the important bit: 40 per cent of the time people did not resume the task they were working on before they were interrupted.

And, worse, the more complex the task, the less likely the person was to return to it.

They don't return to their deep work; they never get back in Flow. They pick up something easier, a lower-value fieldmouse.

When we do get back in Flow we are soon bumped out of it again. Researcher Gloria Mark at the University of California found that people work no more than 12 minutes and 18 seconds before the next interruption. They usually do about two other tasks before they re-orient back to their original activity. The most common intervening task of course is sending an email, which interrupts someone else, who then replies, so you get more emails and so it goes on.

Mark found that people learned to speed up to cope. They completed their interrupted tasks in the right time with no difference in quality. They were still productive. Fabulous. But the trade-off for speed is not so fabulous. The constant time pressure lead to greater frustration and stress. Classic, corrosive Crazy Busyness.

How do you manage interruptions?

You could hide at home or in a meeting room, but if you are collocated, (i.e. people can see you) they'll get a vibe of when it's not a good time to distract you.

It's better to proactively get on top of this by communicating when's good for you. Build some boundaries to ring-fence the time when you are interruptible and protect the time when you aren't.

CLUSTER TIME WHEN YOU CAN BE INTERRUPTED

One of my clients, Avi, was a director of a small consulting business. His priority was to generate new business for the firm, as well as managing a team and informally mentoring others.

New business wasn't coming in because he spent his entire week firefighting, dealing with existing clients and hand-holding his team. He liked to be needed, so it flattered his ego that people wouldn't make decisions without him. He was hard to get hold of because he was always rushing from one demand to another. Consequently, he was preventing other people from making progress on their projects because they needed to talk to him.

His role was measured on new business revenue. He complained he couldn't do this because his team interrupted him so much, he had no time to do his job. He was frustrated, his team was frustrated, his CEO was highly frustrated.

Avi did two things:

1. **Daily 'surgeries':** He made himself available after 4 pm every single day, so people knew they could come with queries then and he'd have time to listen to them. He forced himself to shut his screen, turn his chair around, fix a smile, and give them undivided attention.

   It wasn't always easy for him to be present in the office and available every day, but he managed to make it happen with very few exceptions and, most importantly, to stick to the new routine. It's no good doing this for a few days then slinking back to your old habits: that's going to destroy trust.

2. **Regular check-ins:** Avi also booked short but frequent 1:1 catch-ups with his team, often 20-minute stand-ups, in between more formal meetings. He knew what everyone was doing and that they were all on the right track. They had airtime with him. He was able to identify potential issues before they escalated.

The results were obvious and immediate. By scheduling more time *with* his team, he had more time *away* from them. By and large, they learnt to leave him alone because they had the reassurance of knowing when he would be available to them. He could get on with his priorities during the rest of the day and meet his own targets.

Decent communication enabled him to become a better manager. With his guidance and encouragement, his team learnt to think for themselves, improved their skills and relied on him less. In time, he was able to cut back on some of the 1:1s because they weren't so necessary. They loved him for giving them whole-hearted attention and his appraisal rating for leadership improved.

Prevent most unwanted interruptions by making a big deal of the time when you are available.

I've instigated this across entire teams who have business partnering roles, like HR departments and inhouse lawyers. They were constantly on call, so they had no time to do their work. They scheduled times during the week when they were available and happy to help: 'Come and see us after 11 am every day and we'll always make time to help you.' They expected the announcement to cause friction. In reality, people saw this as a positive announcement that they were there to help. Occasionally senior people bypassed the system but most stuck to it.

PICK WHO TO PLEASE

You can't say 'yes' to everything because time is finite. You might want to please everyone, but you can't. If you are managing others, they need to trust that you will control the work they have to do too, not say 'yes' to everything.

It's crucial that you can identify the activities that will drive real value and say 'no' to the ones that won't. This means choosing between the random curveballs that routinely come your way or more substantial Head Space projects you are offered.

Here's how to weigh up the value of the extra work:

- Is it part of your job? What you are actually paid to do?
- Is it something a high-performer in your role would do?
- Is it career-enhancing, adding to your brand and reputation?
- Is it interesting, fun, challenging, different, lucrative?
- Does it give you access to new networks, stakeholders or skills?
- Is it the best use of your skillset or could you make a more valuable contribution further up? (That's something to think about for charitable/pro-bono efforts – should you build the shelter, or would you have more impact if you fund-raised the project?)

Say 'no' to the request, not the person

Here are some suggestions for how to decline tasks and maintain a positive relationship. Teach your colleagues these tactics too.

State your position firmly and, if possible, signpost other options:

- **Someone is trying to fob something off on you that you have no intention of doing – say 'no' firmly:** *I'd really love to help, but we simply don't have capacity.* **You might want to offer alternative people/teams/solutions but don't over-explain why you aren't doing it**.
- **An important client/stakeholder, who you don't want to upset, is creating unnecessary extra work that you don't think adds value:** *Can we just take a step back here? How can we achieve the outcome you want from this within the scope of our original plan and the tasks already scheduled?*
- **You have multiple execs giving you work – push back and make them communicate with each other to sort it out:** *I'd like to do this for you but I've already agreed to talk to this supplier for Annie. Can you talk to her about which should take priority and let me know?*
- **It's a reasonable request but you can't do it straight away. If you push back they might do it themselves:** *What's the latest you need it by?* **Ask the opposite when you want someone to do something for you:** *What's the soonest you can do it by?*
- **You are supposed to collaborate with this person, but the work they want you to do doesn't fit with your own priorities:** *Can we take a step back here, I understand what you are trying to achieve but I wonder if there's another way of getting that result? Can we schedule 30 minutes to think through all the options?*
- **Someone wants your attention NOW:** *I'm right up against a deadline, I'll come over to you as soon as I am done. I can't do it now, can you come back in 30 minutes?*

Don't spend five minutes explaining why you haven't got five minutes. And it's never five minutes anyway!

PRE-EMPTING FREQUENT INTERRUPTERS

You get the same request multiple times or at the last minute, disrupting your own schedule. These are usually from competitively crazy busy people who are a whirlwind of chaos.

Their requests are always last-minute, 7 am texts asking for information for their 9 am meeting. Sometimes you just have to do it, because they are too senior to decline. If they planned better, then wouldn't always be rushing but it's probably not career-enhancing for you to spell that out.

Here's the magic phrase to take back control:
'I've noticed ...'

- *I've noticed that you often need data for upcoming client meetings. Why don't we touch base weekly, to see what you've got coming up, so I can prepare the information in more detail for you?*

- *I've noticed that you often change what you want in the slide deck just before we present it. How about we always schedule in just 15 minutes to run through it the afternoon before the pitch, so we've got time to get it just right for you?*

- *I've noticed that a few of our projects have changed scope in the middle and I think it would help all of us if we spent more time at the briefing stage. Can we allocate a longer meeting with all stakeholders right at the start to get it just right for you?*

'For you' is a nice way to conclude – the person hears that last and it sounds like you are suggesting this just to improve their lives.

ESTABLISH THE BOUNDARIES

If you, or someone in your team, breaks a process or rule to accommodate someone then they will trample over your boundaries in future. If expenses need to be in by the 20th of the month in order to be paid by the end of that month, then that's the rule. If you break it just once, to be nice, then how can you stick to it in future? No fuzzy boundaries.

The next chapter deals with one of my pet hates ...

CHAPTER 12

What Aristotle would say about cat videos

● ● ●

- Are you connected busy: easily seduced by your favourite apps and social media?
- Do you check your phone constantly, even when you go to the bathroom?

'Attention isn't just about what you're doing right now. It's about the way you navigate your whole life; it's about who you are, who you want to be and the way you define and pursue those things.'
James Williams, ex Google Strategist now Oxford Academic and
expert on tech ethics

Greek philosophers, like Plato and Aristotle, saw freedom from the need to work – leisure time – as the goal of human existence. Leisure would lead to contemplation and virtue, the highest forms of human flourishing, called eudaimonia.

What would they think of how, over 2,500 years on, human civilization has evolved to the point of sharing over 3.8 million cat videos each day? Is this all we aspire to?

Unless your job is to use social media for your business, and you are tracking it carefully, social media use is a serious threat to your productivity and wellbeing. There's plenty of debate already on the damage to our mental health caused by these platforms. Social media use comes up all the time too when I ask people what gets in the way of their productivity. Emails and meetings are usually top, but app addiction is right up there.

Smartphones were originally a source of wonderful information and connection, so every time a thought crossed our mind, who's that guy in the movie, what are the ingredients for goulash and so on, we got an immediate answer or response. We had an abundance of knowledge at our fingertips.

We are addicted to this immediate information (or misinformation) and constant distractions. It's a symptom, or maybe even part of the cause, of the instant gratification society in which we live.

I send my teenage son off to school with a piece of equipment that's worth the best part of a thousand pounds, the same model as all his friends have. I don't want to sound like a dinosaur here, but why are we giving our children their own personal and very expensive amusement arcades, full of pointless distraction and misinformation?

Recently, I've coached a couple of brave people who have reverted to earlier generation phones, dumbphones even, in order to control their app addictions. They both said they'd been accused, kind of jokingly, of being drug-dealers or adulterers with a burner phone. They also confessed that they still kept their apps on their iPads, but they felt much more in control of their time because they didn't feel so constantly available and trackable. They had single-mindedly ditched the connected busyness anyway.

I really should dig one of these out of the kitchen drawer myself. But I'm a sucker for the sleekest, lightest, sexiest phone, who isn't? I couldn't give up my Audible or Spotify subscriptions and I'm a podcast junkie. I just want to control my phone rather than have it control me.

We are being exploited

Tech companies fight for our attention and it would take super-human amounts of willpower to fight their algorithms. We are compelled to come back and play a game so we can reach the next level. Our attention is grabbed by targeted ads and persuasive notifications.

Reed Hastings, CEO of Netflix, has famously described sleep as one of his company's main competitors. This might explain why we feel so wired and tired. Netflix doesn't compete with apps anyway because we're still checking our phones while watching it. Watching a single screen, no phone near us, seems like a huge breakthrough.

FIFTY MINUTES

That's the average amount of time Facebook said, in 2016, that its 1.65 billion users spend each day on its platforms: Facebook, Instagram and Messenger. I'm sure it's gone up since then.

Fifty minutes doesn't sound too bad, does it? But, as James B. Stewart wrote in *The New York Times*, there are only 24 hours in a day, and the average person sleeps for 8.8 of them. (Lucky them.) That means more than one-sixteenth of the average user's waking time is spent on Facebook! That's a lot of wasted Head Space.

I can't imagine what Facebook tries to sell to us, or learn about us, in that precious time. Time means everything to social media companies – the longer we are on, the more engaged and captive we are. Social media uses us, not the other way round.

I came off Facebook a couple of years ago. I'd like to tell you that this is because of the damage it has done to global parliamentary democracy. In part it was.

In truth though, I deleted my account mainly because I have way too many exes and stalking them was becoming too time-consuming.

Honestly, do you ever feel better about yourself when you've been on Facebook?

You know that old joke about people on their death beds regretting the amount of time they spent at work? It's due an update.

What could you do in the time that you spend on social media?

How else could you spend those quiet moments?

_____

_____

_____

_____

_____

YOUR PHONE IS A CONSTANT DISTRACTION

We've talked about switch costs – the time it takes to regain focus once we have been distracted. We don't cluster our phone use, so the switch costs really add up. Research company dscout found that people touch their phones an average of 2,617 times per day. For the 'top 10 per cent of users' the number doubles to 5,427 touches per day. That's about one million touches per year and 2.42 hours of phone screen time per day, rising to 3.75 hours for the most addicted. Hours wasted, lost forever and countless minutes on top, trying to regain our focus.

Just having your phone next to you is a problem. Dr Adrian Ward at the University of Texas found that the mere *presence* of one's smart phone can adversely affect our working memory capacity. Tell that to your kids when they do homework with their phone next to them.

Cluster social media

You can't fight these tech giants. Their whole existence is based on grabbing our attention. You are probably rolling your eyes at this, but please think about whether you can discipline your phone use a bit more.

I try to keep my phone away from me when I am working to beat my Pavlovian response to it. If my phone's not next to me I can't pick it up.

Managing attention

If you are managing others you now have to manage their attention too. If people are overwhelmed, probe their app use.

LinkedIn and social media for use for work

I joined LinkedIn in 2006 when I was working as a recruiter. I benefitted from the access it gave me to a global talent network. I know that I benefit from the worldwide audience the platform gives me as a coach and speaker. LinkedIn is a game-changing way to connect with people and build relationships.

However, as I explain at length in my career book *Mind Flip*, enduring and profitable relationships are built offline. LinkedIn, Twitter etc. are just one touch point and an easy way of staying loosely connected and lightly informed. Real business connection is done through conversations, either virtually or in person.

We can all spend too much time scrolling through feeds and kidding ourselves that this is work. Is it? If social media is your actual job, then it probably is. If it isn't, ask yourself if social media is really the best way to reach your audience or customer? Is there a quicker, better way? Like picking up the phone to a lapsed contact and saying that you just wondered how they were doing?

If your clients are mostly on LinkedIn, do you need to spend hours curating a Facebook or Instagram page as well? Checking other platforms will tell you what your customers think, or more about the people you want to do business with, but once you've taken the temperature you don't have to stay scrolling through feeds.

What matters most to you?

I have met many mediocre managers who always have a phone or two in their hands and spend a lot of time commenting on posts and getting into online spats. I know many super successful people who barely have a social media presence. I doubt that's a coincidence.

CHAPTER 13

The dopamine hit of a list

• • •

- Do you have a long to-do list that never gets done?
- Are you transferring your list from one day to another?
- Or have you just given up writing one altogether?

You may not be a list person, but some kind of daily system helps to anchor you in the fog of overwhelm. It's much easier to keep track of what you've done and what you have to do if you keep a list, and who doesn't love the dopamine hit you get when you tick things off? I've added things I've already done onto my list just for the pleasure of striking them out again.

The to-do list

A good old-fashioned to-do list is especially helpful if you are working from home and distracted by all the home stuff as well as work. Lists thread together your priorities to preserve some structure.

Three reasons why you need a to-do list:

1. **To prevent procrastination:** Having a list of tasks stops you procrastinating over what to do next. You come out of a meeting, check your list and get straight on to the next task. This removes the element of choice: the options of picking up your phone, sending emails or getting lost on the web. You have half an hour to spare, so you get on with field-mice to fill it. You don't lose time identifying a field mouse – they are on your list waiting for you.

2. **To feel in control:** When we have too much to do, we get very little done. We freeze. If you've got a manageable list, you have prioritized where you should focus next. Leadership expert Peter Bregman describes this as breaking down 'the fog of overwhelm'.

   The greater the options, the more difficult it becomes to choose a single one, so we end up choosing none. This applies to the overwhelm of a stuffed schedule, as well as so much else in life – less is definitely more.

   I have a master list of everything I want to do, but keep my daily to-do list as short as I can. One antelope ideally, and a few field mice on a Post-it note.

3. **To focus.** Remember the Zeigarnik effect in the PIMP model? We remember unfinished or interrupted tasks rather than completed ones. Having a list of small stuff, and a plan for when we do them, helps to calm the mind so we can focus on our more important tasks or just clock off and take a break.

WHERE LISTS GO WRONG

If one of your team is really struggling with time management, ask to see their to-do list. That will give you a fair indication of what's going wrong.
   Here are the most common problems I find when I ask to see a client's daily to-do list:

- They don't have one.
- They have one, but it is over-stuffed and probably on a screen, not paper. It takes up several pages and it's a chore in itself to transfer it from one day/week to the next. Invariably they stop bothering.
- They have a manageable list but no daily priorities. Each task is given equal weight. If they run out of time, they've cracked into the small stuff only, so will be mega-stressed.

Steps to structure your to-do list

These recap points covered in earlier chapters – but applying them to your to-do list will reap benefits:

- Identify your personal goals. They should dovetail nicely with your organizational objectives, your boss's agenda and your own values. What do you want to achieve? Personally and professionally too.
- Break these down these into achievable steps and milestones.
- These chunks become your antelopes – priority tasks. This is your master to-do list, a list of everything you need to do under each topic or goal heading. I have annual and monthly ones.
- PIMP your calendar, matching these priorities/antelopes to your time, so you have a viable action plan to getting them done, rather than just a hopeful intention.
- Now write a daily or weekly to-do list, reflecting these antelopes and the small field mice to fit in around the sides when you get a gap: the calls, admin, chores. Can any of these easier, small tasks overlap with appropriate multitasking? Easy admin while you listen to a podcast, making quick calls when you go out to get lunch that save you a backwards and forwards email conversation, or you go for an uninterrupted walk when you can make a longer call.

LIST TIMING AND TECHNOLOGY

Find a system that works for you. I schedule three hours every Friday to plan, update my master to-do list and catch up on any admin. I always do a daily list, usually on a Post-it or small piece of card that I can keep visible. I always ask myself what the *one* thing I need to get done that day is, and make sure I've PIMPed the time into my calendar to do it.

TECH OR RETRO LISTS?

There are umpteen apps for creating to-do lists. Evernote, OneNote, Google Tasks, Todoist, Wunderlist, Any.do and Remember the Milk are just a few. Experiment to find a system that you find easy to keep up. If they make your life more complex, then don't bother.

WORKFLOW MANAGEMENT

In 2019, I went to Sloan Business School at MIT in Boston for a course on dynamic work design. I wanted to understand the very latest thinking in improving work processes at an organizational level.

Expecting that I'd have to learn complicated new technology, I waited apprehensively to learn Professor Nelson Repenning's world-renowned process improvement framework.

I was enormously relieved when he chucked Post-it notes and sharpies at us and told us to use flip charts to draw out the workflow glitches in our case studies. Of course! Using stick men and wiggly lines, we were able to map out entire projects and could immediately see at which stage they were going wrong.

As Nelson said, we'd fixed the productivity blockers in way less time than it would take to even scope out an expensive software tool.

There are plenty of tools out there for collaborative projects – Trello is popular. I'm sure you use one or more right now. Just don't ignore the ease of old school visual mapping. When I get my clients to plot their team processes on a whiteboard, any bottlenecks or unequal distribution of work are immediately visible and fixable.

That's the tactical stuff out the way. Now, how do we get in our own way?

CHAPTER 14

Quit faffing and trying to be perfect

• • •

- Do you delay starting tasks, fixing to get ready rather than just start-ing them?
- Do you just … check your emails, … check your phone, … make another cup of tea before starting something?
- Do you chase every possible field mouse before you start on your antelope?

Why do we faff about, distract ourselves and delay starting the tasks we need to get on with?

If a task isn't scheduled, it doesn't get done

We've covered, at length, how to schedule time and location in order to get your priorities done, including following the PIMP process to min-imize choice and distractions. We know about Parkinson's Law, which we can control by setting timers and strict guidelines about how long a task should take so we don't take too long to do it.

Are you still faffing around rather than getting on with it?

Use the following list to focus your efforts:

1. Don't get overwhelmed
If I have three substantial things to do then I get on with them, if I have a longer to-do list then it feels so unmanageable that I struggle to do

any of them. Three works for me and gives me the energy to do lots of field mice around the sides.

Dr Sheena Iyengar, of Colombia University Business School, did a fascinating experiment to illustrate how too many choices stops us from making decisions. A group of people was offered samples of six different jams available for purchase, while another group was presented with 24 different jams. The six-jam group was ten times more likely to actually purchase a jam because they weren't lost in a fog of overwhelm. Pick the few antelopes with the greatest impact.

2. Watch your perfectionist tendencies

Many of my clients are insecure high achievers, who put pressure on themselves to be perfect. Procrastinator is a big red flag of perfectionism.

Think about it. You've got an important report to write, due in by Friday morning. If you plan time early in the week to write and edit it, you stand a fair chance of producing a decent quality document. If you do it over Thursday night and the early hours of Friday morning, you are giving yourself a get-out clause for a sub-standard result: 'If I only had more time, it would have been perfect.'

You are protecting yourself from the fear of failure. If you'd wholeheartedly thrown yourself into writing the report, and it still wasn't up to your uncompromisingly high standards, you'd have to deal with that. This way, your perfectionist tendencies have held you back, protecting you from facing up to your perceived sub-standard performance and failures.

Rather than giving you a safety net, the avoidance behaviour creates even more stress and anxiety. Your delaying and last-minute approach likely creates stress for the people waiting for the work downstream.

Perfectionists can be created when they are criticized as children for less than perfect performance: the one spelling they got wrong, not the nineteen they got right.

Life is just too full now to do everything perfectly. Some jobs need to be perfect; some just need to get over the line. Reduce the pressure you put on yourself and know when good enough is absolutely fine.

What you choose to do is significantly more important than how you do it.

PART 3

Staying productive

CHAPTER 15

Don't wait to feel motivated, just start

• • •

- Are some days more productive than others?
- Does your motivation dip?
- Does what you do depend on how you feel?

Curing Crazy Busyness is about making the right choices about what you do and when and how you do it. Before we explore the effect of our fluctuating moods, I want to go back in history and get some lessons from the Industrial Revolution about morale. Specifically, how we have forgotten the most basic lesson in human motivation: the impact of worker autonomy on productivity.

The economic and motivational damage of Crazy Busyness

When I run Crazy Busy reboot sessions for leaders, I start by getting them to imagine they are running a manufacturing assembly line and to compare that to how they work in reality. How often do they stop the line because someone interrupts them? How much time do they spend in meetings talking about what should be assembled rather than actually getting on with it?

The assembly line achieves maximum efficiency because of its rigidly defined procedures. Not a moment is wasted switching from one task to another.

As well as the precision in every aspect of the tasks, the advantage of the process is it isn't mood dependent. You just get on with it. Each worker is just a cog, a replaceable part of a complex whole. This system of synthesizing business processes was first advocated by American mechanical engineer Frederick Winslow Taylor. His 1911 book, *The Principles of Scientific Management*, applied his engineering principles to management.

In Taylorism, the factory manager had to break down each job into its individual motions, work out which ones were essential and then time the workers with a stopwatch to eliminate any unnecessary movement. The worker, following this robotic routine, called 'the one best way', was much more effective because they didn't have to choose what to do next. They just did what was put in front of them by their manager.

Taylor was probably the first management consultant and his ideas were revolutionary, if contentious. His methods were highly criticized because making work so monotonous alienated and demoralized workers.

We may have left the industrial revolution far behind, but workers are still bored out of their brains. According to Gallup, 85 per cent of employees are either not engaged or are actively disengaged at work. The economic consequences of this global 'norm' are approximately $7 trillion in lost productivity. 18 per cent are actively disengaged in their work and workplace, while 67 per cent are 'not engaged'. Whilst not all of these employees will be plonked in front of a screen all day, many of them are.

Too many of them still run on autopilot: responding to what's right in front of them like those bored assembly line workers. Only this time, they are processing emails. They still aren't making active choices about what they do next.

Can we learn anything from the line?

There's still elements we can take from Taylor. His managers were the first Lawn Mower managers (coming up in Chapter 19).

I'm all in favour of reintroducing Time and Motion studies too. We need to know how long it takes to actually do our core tasks to do the Head Space model. I'm not sure standing over people with a stopwatch would be acceptable these days, but we can certainly track performance on a timesheet to get the data as a starting point.

What drives a person's choice of what they do and how hard they will work at it?

Motivation remains a very complex subject that is at the heart of making productive choices. It drives our choice of what to do next.

Most of us are rewarded on results, not effort. Managers talk much more about end results and outcomes, assume the person has the tools and competence to do the work, and don't spend enough time breaking it down into measurable chunks that they can give feedback on.

Feedback is essential to keep motivation going

Psychologists Dr Edwin Locke and Dr Gary Latham spent many years researching the theory of goal setting. They believe that feedback is essential to keeping us motivated and on track. It's not the end point that inspires us, it's the progress towards it. Once we've cleared debts and achieved some traction in our careers, pay and rewards are only considered as motivators because they count as more feedback data. They give us a benchmark as to how well we are doing. What's that old joke? Money doesn't matter to me as long as I earn more than my brother in law.

Closing the feedback loop to correct our performance is more satisfactory and motivational than completing the goal.

It's always easier to coach the silver medallist than the gold: they know the gap and how to close it. That feedback is what motivates them to keep going, not completing the task. The Gold medallist is looking around for their next challenge.

If you've handed in a dissertation or completed a project you may recognize the sense of emptiness that follows that initial feeling of euphoria. I delayed the last thousand words of this book, to my publisher's irritation, until I had decided on the next book I want to write.

How to get feedback to stay motivated and adjust your performance

- PIMP time once a week to analyse your progress.
- Ask for feedback from people who will give you critical, objective and challenging support – coaches, trusted colleagues and managers.
- Say 'thank you', even if you disagree with it.
- Break your task down into chunks and give yourself deadlines you can tick off as you meet them.
- Listen to unsolicited feedback. Read between the lines about what people say about you and your work. What are your blind spots?

Mood is irrelevant, just do it

Motivation is the driver of what you choose to do next, but sometimes we just aren't in the mood. We know what we should do, we are motivated to do it, we can choose when we will attempt it, we just don't feel like it. We procrastinate, dither around, get sucked in a vortex of digital distractions. We do anything rather than face the discomfort of getting on with what we have to do.

We say we're not in the mood and we'll start it when we are. Actually, that's not true. We just don't *feel* like it right now.

Most schools make the children do their maths lesson when it is timetabled, not when they feel like it. We need the same professionalism and structure as a six-year-old.

Moods and feelings are different and often confused. Moods can last hours or even days and are a response to all sorts of external and internal factors: the people around us, environmental factors, what we eat or drink, how we've exercised, and our own mental state. Several friends in lockdown described their mood to me as 'low' and they couldn't put their finger on exactly why, although there was clearly a number of causes.

Feelings are how we interpret our emotions and are much shorter-term than mood. We respond to a trigger, like someone senior wanting a word later in the day, and a chemical is released in our brain which causes an emotion. We synthesize that emotion into a feeling. That request from a senior person might make you feel anxious, or delighted, depending on how you rate your recent performance.

The feeling is much more short-term than a mood. You can feel anxious, but your mood can be generally much more positive. But your anxious feeling can stop you choosing to get on with your work, you faff around on other things, delay your critical tasks until much later in the day, and create a cycle of unhealthy behaviour.

The good news is that there are easy ways to positively distract yourself and get back on track, irrespective of how you feel. Here's a recap, under the theme 'just do it'.

- Know your antelopes and stick to your PIMP schedule to do them.
- Remove the element of choice by allocating time in your schedule. Stick to your prompt to begin the task, even if you don't feel like it.

- Keep to a list, so when you finish one task you move on to the next one in your list.
- Keep that list short. Remember Sheena Iyengar's jam research? Too many options overwhelm us. Cut your daily list down to a manageable number. Keep your long wish list to refer to.
- Start where you feel comfortable to get your energy and confidence up.
- Starting it means allowing yourself time to figure out how to actually do it: gaining support, making a plan, scoping it out. Don't rush it.
- Treat yourself to a scrolling session through your favourite apps when you FINISH the task, not during it.

Weekly questions to keep your energy up

Here's a series of reflexive questions I encourage my clients to ask at the start of every week to ensure they retain a laser-focus on chasing those antelopes. You can go through them on your own, with a coach, or with your team, whatever works best.

What were the highlights of last week? Any lessons learnt?

_____

What three things need to happen this week for it to be a success?

_____

What am I avoiding or making hard for myself?

_____

What is it only I can do?

_____

Who can I delegate to and who needs to be upskilled for this to happen?

_____

Which relationships do I need to invest time in?

_____

Who do I need to connect with?

_____

What do I need to deal with now, to save me a bigger headache later?

_____

If I felt I couldn't fail, what would I do next?

_____

Given all that, what's my greatest priority this week and when am I going to get it done?

_____

Rattle through the questions. If you are doing this with your team don't do a post-mortem on last week. You just need to know which fires to fight first this week and what you can ignore for now.

Reflection increases productivity

Taking time away from the desk to think like this is not an indulgence. It is proven to increase productivity. A 2017 article in the *Harvard Business Review* cited a study finding that when people added 15 minutes of reflection into the end of their workday, as opposed to working an extra 15 minutes, their productivity increased by nearly a *quarter* in just ten days. When reassessed a month later, that spike in productivity had stuck.

There's no excuse now – you can power through your priorities, but if you are still struggling there may be some causes beneath the surface.

CHAPTER 16

Invisible productivity problems

• • •

- Do you think you struggle more than most people to get organized?
- Do you find it difficult to pay attention or sit still, even for short periods?
- Does your mind drift off when getting verbal instructions?

I tried to keep the cures straightforward and would love to know which ones help you the most. Some people find it harder than others to break out of our Crazy Busy habits.

It's estimated that about one in seven people in the UK, that's more than 15 per cent of the population, are neurodivergent, (ACAS). That means that their brain processes information in a different way to the rest of us. Neurodivergence includes attention deficit disorders, autism, dyslexia, dyspraxia and other neurological conditions, like brain injuries.

Each form of neurodivergence varies from individual to individual, and not all fit the stereotypes. Not all autistic people are maths geniuses for example, but many bring passion and intense focus to the workplace.

Managers are waking up to the needs of neurodiverse colleagues for tailored support. It's called cognitive accessibility. For example, some autistic people like to work with noise cancelling headphones and prefer calm office environments and structured routines.

ACAS estimate that only 17 per cent of organizations know how many neurodivergent individuals are within their organization. Some people have less obvious needs, but their strengths can go hand in hand with some kind of processing disorder. You could call them hidden disabilities.

You may be secretly struggling with personal organization, or perhaps you are aware of colleagues who are. If you are puzzled why your super-clever Oxbridge intern or maths graduate is frequently late, doesn't seem to listen to you, appears chaotic and struggles to finish tasks, please don't write them off. They might have some hidden processing or regulation issues. They need your help to contribute to their full, very high, potential.

I have some insider knowledge about dyspraxia, for example. Dyspraxic people have difficulties with tasks requiring sequencing, structure, organization and timekeeping. Their extra strategic and creative thinking ability can fool others into thinking that they are merely 'disorganized'.

These people need extra help from you to help them plan and organize their activities. That's the reason why I like coloured paper and pens: I'm very visual and long lists on a screen just swim in front of me. My daughter is extremely dyspraxic and I suspect I have an element of it too. There's definitely something going on.

I struggle with left and right, have no sense of direction and my map-reading skills are infamous. I had a brief and undistinguished early career in the WRNS, the Women's Royal Naval Service. Women didn't go to sea in those days, we couldn't be trusted with all those sailors apparently. As a junior and eager Wren Writer, I was sent to participate behind the scenes in an actual NATO exercise on a navy base in Rosyth, Scotland. I plotted HMS *Arethusa* smack bang in the middle of Spain where it rested for ten minutes or so before someone asked, in salty naval language, exactly what it was doing there. I had got my eastings and northings very confused. (We had to work this stuff out ourselves in the days before Google Maps.) I was swiftly taken off that task for good and sent to make a round of tea.

Before she was diagnosed as dyspraxic at 16, my daughter Alannah's teachers got frustrated that an intelligent child could be so chaotic – losing kit, ID cards and keys, missing essay deadlines, struggling with getting to classes on time, overcome with lassitude and so on. It wasn't her 'fault'. She struggles to process this stuff because she has a biological disorder, not a behavioural problem.

Now she has worked out her own strategies, like allowing extra time to get organized. Even her proud mother can see that detailed project planning is unlikely to be her main skillset. However, she has a gift of seeing solutions to complex problems more quickly than others. Her brain seems to skip straight to the end result, then fill in the details from there. That's an asset, as long as someone checks in with her to ask her what she might have missed.

How can you help if you spot problems in others?

It's safe to assume that everyone wants to do their best work and, if you see that people are struggling with personal organization, it is not always a case of 'could try harder'.

Alannah's diagnosis was immensely reassuring and enabled her to come up with both an explanation and coping strategies. She's very lucky. There are many people in the workplace who haven't had that luxury. They know something isn't quite right, but think they are just stupid (as they may have been told in the past). They may not even have had a formal diagnosis, but they know that they struggle with things other people appear to find easy. This can lead to stress and shame: hardly conducive to productivity or motivation.

Some gentle coaching from you could help them find workable solutions:

- Make it easy for them to talk to you about it.
- As ever with feedback, don't make it personal – 'you're chaotic' – keep it specific to the task.
- They'll know what works for them and a conversation with a manager, and maybe an occupational health referral, will give them the space to figure out how to put reasonable adjustments in place. Sometimes there are fairly obvious solutions, like ring-fencing time, setting a timer as a prompt, giving them a white board to map out their work, or finding the right app.
- Their brain can work against them to work out this kind of detail themselves (that's the irony). One hour of coaching from you to support them will earn you incalculable loyalty. You aren't qualified to give a diagnosis, but you can point out where you've seen they need support.

THE CRAZY BUSY CURE

- Acknowledge the issue and move on to the solution: Use my 'I have noticed' phrase to start the conversation tactfully:

  ○ *'I have noticed that you rarely dial in to our weekly meetings on time, what do you need to help you do this?'*

  ○ *'I have noticed that you seem to lose things a lot, which must be frustrating for you. Can we brainstorm some ideas to help you?'*

  ○ *'I have noticed that you often miss deadlines, do you need a visual reminder of what's coming up so you can stay on track? Can we brainstorm ideas?'*

  ○ *'I've noticed that you don't volunteer to work on new group projects, I wondered if there are any contributions you would like to make that would allow you to work mostly on your own. Could we have a chat about it?'*

Encouraging neurodiverse talent should be a top-down initiative in organizations. Managers should be trained to support individuals to maximize their contribution. That means relishing their strengths and different perspectives, not highlighting their weak spots.

We've got to become better at talking about all mental health issues at work and supporting each other. People want to talk, but they might not know who to talk to. Remind people of sources of support in your organization at every opportunity, so when the day comes that they need help, they know where to go immediately.

CHAPTER 17

Zoom zombies and flexible working

• • •

- Do you find it harder to concentrate when you work from home or are you much more productive?
- Are virtual meetings more tiring than physical ones?
- Does your mood fluctuate from day to day when you are away from the office?

Why is virtual work so draining?

As COVID-19 lockdown threatened, I bought Hilary Mantel's latest book, *The Mirror and the Light*, assuming I'd have ample time to get lost in its 754 pages. I still haven't read a word of it, but it's a very handy size to balance my laptop on for a better camera angle on Zoom. What happened to my focus?

My monkey brain was in control.

Our monkey, limbic brains went into survival mode as we grappled with economic, health and emotional pressures. We may have felt in control on the surface, but our subconscious minds were working overtime in 'flight or fight' mode. That's why many of us remembered vivid dreams, as our limbic, subconscious brain worked round the clock trying to protect ourselves and our loved ones from external threats. It was very hard to concentrate for long periods.

Instead of setting myself two-hour blocks of Flow working, I just PIMPed in an hour, or even 45 minutes – intensive bursts rather than longer blocks.

Too much or too little to do?

People with less to do than normal discover Parkinson's Law: tasks expand to fill the time available. They take as long to do four tasks as they take to do ten. Others with more on their plate, including caring responsibilities, have that paradoxical fog of overwhelm that comes with too many choices (remember Sheena Iyengar's jam experiment?). They have too much to do and can't get anything done at all.

Managers in this kind of crisis need to adjust workloads to reflect what's going on: spread the load round more evenly and clarify priorities.

The decision to work from home during the pandemic was out of our control.

Between 2010 and 2015, psychologists Neel Doshi and Lindsay McGregor surveyed more than 20,000 workers in more than 50 companies around the world to figure out what motivates people, including how much working from home made a difference to them. When they measured motivation of people working from home versus the office, they found that working from home was *less* motivating, especially when they had no choice in where they worked. This is what has happened to us when we locked down. There was no choice.

Doshi and McGregor found that total motivation dropped so much when remote working was forced on them, it was the equivalent of moving from one of the best to one of the unhappiest cultures in the world.

I often work from home; it's a huge perk of being self-employed. However, I'm used to it being just me and the dog. I'm not used to my family being here all day, competing for the wi-fi, using up the milk and showering noisily when I'm about to go live.

How do you stay engaged and motivated working virtually?

This is the advice I gave leaders and teams during lockdown. Here it is again. I hope the lockdown threat has passed, but it is still relevant to keeping any virtual teams engaged and motivated:

ZOOM ZOMBIES: VIRTUAL MEETING MANAGEMENT

- Virtual work is exhausting because we have to concentrate much harder to pick up all the non-verbal cues. Reassess your meeting schedule and cut back if you can. Ask people what would work better for them. Cap meeting lengths to keep them pacey.

- Separate wellbeing meetings from the business ones, otherwise people feel that you are just paying lip-service to the emotional aspects, waiting to get on to the real agenda.

- The novelty of Zoom socials has definitely worn off. Double-check if people really want to do them. When we keep inviting work into home it means the boundaries between the two get fuzzy. It might be kinder to give introverts a break from their screens, or at least make your socials optional. One team I work with agree that all videos are on, or all videos are off, at the start of each meeting. It's not easy to have equal influence in a meeting if your camera is off when most people have theirs on. If you really don't want to be seen, or audio-only connection is better, then make an extra effort to get your points across. Can you dial in on your phone if that gives you a better connection?

TRAIN FRAZZLED MONKEY BRAINS TO WORK MORE QUICKLY

- Set mini deadlines to stop people procrastinating. Encourage shorter blocks of time.

- Monitor your team's activity and ensure they are having proper breaks. Encourage them to work through their core tasks more efficiently so they get through them in less time and then switch off. That should be the goal here, not pointless presenteeism. Lead by example on this.

- Lunchbreaks are a necessity: make everyone block them out in their calendars. I don't care if people are working across time-zones: they have to have a proper break to re-energize.

- I print off documents to read them quickly (I know, I know) as paper has less distractions.

- Explain to your team how their performance will be measured if they are in an unusual period of virtual work. Quality of output, not quantity of emails, is what should matter.

CLOSER TEAMS ARE MORE PRODUCTIVE

- If you want your team to stay engaged and motivated, give them engaging and motivating work to do.

- What's a game-changing problem no one ever has had time to fix before? Can you start it now?

- Get people collaborating to build team relationships and trust. Set them problems to solve. 'What can we do to make the greatest impact on our customers during this time?'

- Keep checking in with the progress of the work, not checking up on the workers.

- Practise your coaching and feedback skills: how's it going? What are you learning? How did you make that happen? What's working well for you now?

- Seeing an end result gives us a sense of achievement. That's why baking is so popular – people want to see an end result and something they can control. Can you translate that drive into work instead: impactful projects, with clear output?

BUILD YOUR OWN BOUNDARIES AND DON'T PANIC-WORK

- Be wary of your own need to add value or justify your salary if you are working remotely. Don't create work or complexity for the sake of it. If you are going through a quieter phase, enjoy the Head Space.

- If you are combining work and caring responsibilities, try to do one thing at once. You can't work and supervise home schooling at the same time. That's guaranteed burnout right there.

- Get those hard boundaries between work and home in whatever way works for you. Put your work clothes on in the morning and get changed into home gear later. One of my clients leaves through his front door at the end of the day and comes straight back in through the kitchen door. This makes him feel he's psychologically finished for the day.

VISIBILITY IS CREDIBILITY: SHOULD YOU WORK FROM HOME PERMANENTLY?

Most people are way more productive at home. Fewer distractions mean we can knuckle down and think. This proves once and for all how bonkers office life has become: it is hard to do real work at our actual place of work.

Often the choice of how you work comes down to travel. Do you want to stand on a dark Surrey station on a Monday morning in January, clasping an expensive coffee, hoping that the 07.27 to Waterloo turns up?

Wouldn't you be happier if you went for a run first thing, logged on at 08.00 and got an hour of focused work in before your first meeting? Of course you would be.

Are you missing something here though? Does cancelling your commute mean sabotaging your long term career prospects?

WHAT DO YOU TRADE OFF WHEN YOU DITCH THE COMMUTE?

Nicholas Bloom and his colleagues conducted a Working From Home experiment at CTrip, a 16,000 employee NASDAQ listed Chinese travel agency. Call centre employees who volunteered to work from home were randomly assigned to work from home or in the office for nine months. Home working led to a 13 per cent performance increase but the people that were in the office climbed the greasy pole quicker than their more effective colleagues at home. We might be happier and more productive at home, but our careers can suffer. Why is this?

Employees in the office are better known, they have those serendipitous conversations that highlight opportunities, they have better networks, more informal information from spontaneous chats, they are a part of the soul of the office. You can't curate this virtually.

Does cancelling your commute damage your long-term career prospects? Organizations are (mostly) much more capable at remote managing since Bloom's research was done and there'll be plenty of great data as a result of the COVID-19 lockdown. Tools to communicate and monitor performance have improved too. But human factors still apply. We are social animals after all. No matter how creative you are with your tech, there are times when face to face is best for the business and best for your career too. Influencing is much easier in person.

Some tasks are still better executed in a shared physical space, like brainstorming, launching new projects, and building social connections. Contrived chatrooms are merely adequate stand-ins for more revealing, face-to-face conversations. Leaders especially need to turn up if they have staff in the office. You can only truly take the temperature of the team by feeling it yourself. What message does it give if they are in, and you're not?

YOUR WEEK SHOULD BE ACTIVITY DRIVEN

Given that flexible and remote working should be an acceptable option for all of us, from now on where you work should be determined by the activities you need to do. The rhythm of many of our weeks are likely to change to a blend of both work and home.

This will take better planning and assertive communication: you can't have half the team wanting Friday brainstorms when the other half want to stay at home. Flexible working really will mean being flexible: developing a tolerance for changing routines as we adjust our working pattern to meet differing demands and activities.

For concentrating on deep work, stay at home. For a day of 1:1s or client workshops, go into your office or hub. Get your team together physically only when you need to. Make meetings count with pithy agendas and pace. Limit virtual meetings as much as you can – they are exhausting.

If you need to stay at home, then make sure your productivity is rewarded and your career isn't compromised. Keep building trust with your team.

HOW DO YOU MAINTAIN 'CAREER CAPITAL' WHEN YOU WORK VIRTUALLY?

Plenty of people work in virtual, global teams: many of my coaching clients do. However, they still get together in person for conferences and team meetings. If your circumstances mean that's not possible for you then figure out how you can remain visible and involved.

Pick up the phone more often to stay in touch, encourage virtual coffees to know what people are working on and what challenges they are facing. Don't let people make assumptions about your career goals. Push for career conversations to make your contribution and aspirations clear.

Grab opportunities to build networks and relationships. Use your saved commuting time to learn more about your area of expertise and create opportunities to share it.

PART 4

Leading others out of Crazy Busyness

CHAPTER 18

Are you a Control Freak, Superstar or Mother Hen?

• • •

- Have you had training in effective team management?
- What have you delegated from your own job in order to free up time to manage others?
- Who takes up more of your time: your rising stars or under-performers?

Congratulations. Your hard work, possibly your Crazy Busyness, has been recognized. You've been given management responsibilities on top of your existing priorities.

Your team could be new hires, people you inherit or, trickiest of all, people who were peers and are now subordinate to you.

Moving from subject matter expert to a leadership role is a tricky transition. Successful individual contributors can derail when they get people to manage.

I've seen many new managers make the mistake of stumbling into one of these three management styles:

1. **The Control Freak Trap:** Your team are OK, but they have a long way to go. You spend a lot of time with them, checking up on what they are up to and explaining how to do it better next time. Often you end up doing the work for them when they run out of time. To be honest that's easier than explaining it to them anyway.

2. **The Superstar Trap:** You have management responsibilities but are still rewarded and measured mostly on your own performance. Logically, you spend as little time managing as you can get away with.

You have 1:1s every Monday with them then leave them to get on with it for the rest of the week. Some of their performance isn't up to scratch (these snowflakes are so lazy) but you are too busy to instigate a tedious performance management system with them. With a bit of luck, they'll get the hint and bugger off, so you can hire a decent replacement.

3. **The Mother Hen Trap:** You book yourself on a Mindful Management course so you can truly develop the people that work for you. Some of them have been bouncing around the business for a while, delivering lack-lustre results. You are convinced that they'll come good under your wing. You spend hours in meetings with them, asking how they feel about their performance and what they intend to do differently in future. Your own manager wants you to move them out, but you are optimistic that in six months or so you'll turn their performance around. In the meantime, you commit to picking up the slack yourself. You cancel your gym membership and postpone your holiday, so you can devote yourself to 'being the best manager you can be'.

None of these styles work – for you or the people that work for you. They either become overdependent on you or frustrated that you won't let them grow.

Here's how to juggle your own priorities with managing other people:

STEP 1: ELIMINATE SOME OF YOUR OWN WORKLOAD

You were able to devote 100 per cent of your focus and energy to your work before, which is why you have been rewarded with promotion. Something has to go. You can't invent more hours. Negotiate what percentage of your week you are now supposed to spend managing and where you will find that time. What has to go?

This is a dilemma we've all faced. Your own manager should have some helpful insights on how to get the balance right. You can't do everything you did before. Can you change the way you work, so you get through your own priorities more efficiently?

Some tasks can be delegated to your team. They might not do it as well as you, but a manager's job is to manage, not to *do* everything. Get your head round that.

Let go of your need to control everything. Once your employees are trained, skilled and motivated then let them get on with it. Don't duplicate effort by micromanaging them. Get out of their way (more on that in the next chapter).

Successful managers aim to build their team's self-efficacy – belief in their own ability to set high goals and persist in the face of obstacles.

Staying in the weeds is a default behaviour for managers who don't know how to be strategic. Block out some time to figure out what you should be doing instead and get support if necessary.

Don't moan about the workload, other departments, systems, clients, your boss. You are a role model now. Managers should be the most calm, positive and organized people in the room, giving out the vibe that they can handle even more responsibility, so are promotable to the next level.

STEP 2: YOU'RE A MANAGER, SO MANAGE

Commit to the role wholeheartedly, don't shirk from it. 'Manager' isn't just a job title that comes with length of service, it is a new skillset, set of behaviours and frame of mind for you to acquire. Get on it.

The starting point is to ensure everyone in their team knows exactly what they are responsible for, with a crystal-clear job description and key performance indicators.

Always start from scratch with inexperienced hires. Don't waste time assuming that new hires know what they are doing or expect them to be mind-readers.

Managers are encouraged to coach, but you can't coach when people don't know what they are doing yet. You have to teach. When their skills are developed and you understand their strengths, weaknesses and idiosyncrasies, then start coaching them to think for themselves and come up with their own performance improvements.

To start with, show them what to do and how you want it done. I've seen too many people fail because they have been left to get on with things. They run off in the wrong direction, take too long to on-board properly and then get a surprise at the first review point because their performance isn't up to scratch.

No one helped you when you started? Just because you figured this stuff out for yourself doesn't mean everyone else can.

Set clear guidelines too – on personal phone use, hours of work, communication standards, expected behaviours, meeting etiquette and so on. Don't be passive aggressive/sarcastic about it, just be honest about what you want and lead by example.

People respect managers who challenge, inspire and thank them. Obviously be nice to them, but they don't want you to be their best friend. They want you to push them to develop their skills and, ultimately, achieve their career goals.

STEP 3: FEEDBACK LIBERALLY

Feedback should be part of everyday conversations, not saved up for an appraisal. I don't mean unspecific 'awesomes', but telling people what they did well, so they can repeat it.

- *'I really liked how you handled that fee negotiation by breaking down all the components of the service so they could see what they were getting.'*

Don't sandwich feedback old-style (good bit, real message, token positive note to end on) or they will always look for the 'however' section when you praise them. Skip straight to the meat and tell them what you want to tell them.

If you regularly give positive feedback, then negative feedback is no big deal: it's all handed out with a positive intention and is action/behaviour related, never personal. Talk about their behaviour, never their character.

Encourage listening, introspection and learning:

- *'Next time we face the same issues, what can we do to get that result more efficiently?'*
- *'How do you think we can boost this performance?'*

Ask for feedback on your own performance too:

- *'Where could you use more help from me? Where could you use less help now, so I can back off a bit?'*

Conversations don't have to be 'difficult' if all your communication comes with positive intent – usually professional achievement of outcomes. Never make personal comments. Be specific about the behaviours you want to change and nip problems in the bud early on:

- *'I've noticed that you have been late for the team meeting twice in a row, can we have a chat about that?'*

- *'When you come in to work hungover and snappy like this morning, it has a really bad effect on everyone else's mood. It's up to you what you do in your own time, but you need to show up to work and act professionally please. Right, let's crack on with it.'*

- *'I saw that you were reading your emails during the presentation which made me think you aren't very engaged. Is that the case? What's going on?'*

If you have skilled team members whose productivity lapses, then deal with it quickly before the problem escalates. Tell them what you've noticed. Are they stressed? Do they have problems outside work? Or maybe they are just bored and need some additional challenges?

If their work continues to slip, despite your interventions, then talk to HR and put a performance process in place. Don't put your head in the sand. Sometimes the wrong decision is better than no decision.

STEP 4: GET SOME BOUNDARIES

You won't get your own work done if you are constantly interrupted, so put a process in place to make sure your reports don't hijack your time. Ask them in the morning if they have everything they need to get their work done. If you aren't completely confident in their abilities yet, arrange a check-in later in the day ('Let's grab five minutes before lunch to catch up'). This should give you – and them – scheduled time to get on with work without interruptions. This isn't micromanaging, it's coaching and encouraging.

If there are serial interrupters, it could be that you haven't done enough training or standard setting with them. Perhaps they are over-dependent on seeking your approval. Counter-intuitively, more quick, informal conversations WITH them, at a time to suit you, will build their confidence and give you more time AWAY from them. Clinic-style sessions ('I'm free from 4 pm every day if you need my input') will mean you can hold off the constant queries and deal with them in batches, rather than be constantly distracted.

Finally, don't feel you need all the answers or that you know the best way to do other people's job. Your role is to facilitate their thinking, not think for them. Great managers know their strengths, get feedback on their blind spots and aren't frightened to admit when they don't know something or that they have made a mistake.

Now you know the tactics of managing workers, let's make sure you manage the workflow – it's time to learn about the principles of lawn mower management.

CHAPTER 19

Lawn Mower Management

• • •

- How much time do you spend actively managing your people?
- How do you set and communicate priorities?
- What do you want from your team? Do they all know that?

We all know parents who are excessively involved in their children's lives. They clear the path in front of their little darlings, removing obstacles that could impede their success. They are over-involved in their lives: doing their homework, controlling their schedules, hyper-monitoring their activities and, in extreme cases, bribing their teachers. No doubt well intentioned, their meddling prevents their children from experiencing the setbacks and failures that create resilient, high-functioning adults.

This type of parenting is a bad thing.

This type of management is more or less what a manager is supposed to do. I call it Lawn Mower Management. The most important – yet often most neglected – part of a manager's job is simply to clear the path. That means managing workflow so that people can make daily, incremental progress towards their priority tasks. To get on with their work.

The single most powerful motivator at work is simply steady progress towards getting stuff done. That dopamine hit of ticking something off a list.

Equally, the single most demotivating event is the opposite of progress – setbacks in the path to getting work done.

Researchers say steady progress by far outweighs any other motivator like financial incentives or well-being initiatives.

Harvard researchers Teresa Amabile and Steven Kramer analysed nearly 12,000 diary entries provided by 238 employees in seven companies to understand how managers can foster progress and enhance motivation every day. The research found that the single most powerful influence on people's inner-work life was daily small successes.

This progress was the common denominator of success in the thousands of diary entries that the authors collected. The managers who participated in the research actually ranked progress as one of the least important factors of facilitating success. When I ask most managers what they rate as most important about their job, they put a whole bunch of other tasks first too.

There you have it. All you have to do to have higher productivity and great team satisfaction is help people get on with their work! Clear their path and you will get the top feedback scores for your management skills.

Think of all the money you can save on interventions that are good for morale but are pointless if the workflow is still full of bottlenecks.

How do you clear the path?

Facilitating progress should be your number one priority from now. This means sweating the small stuff as well as keeping an eye on the end goal:

- Iron out glitches.
- Speed up decision-making.
- Remove cumbersome processes.
- Prevent duplication of effort.
- Stamp out time-wasting.
- Break down silos.
- Improve communication.
- Enhance meeting structures.
- Build higher functioning teams but maintain individual communication.
- Have fit-for-purpose systems.

Many well-intentioned management activities even *slow down* progress. You get so bogged down in busy stuff that you don't have time to listen or plan. Allowing problems to escalate is a proven de-motivator. We then waste more time managing the demotivation rather than fixing the real problem that caused it.

What activity reports do you ask for each week? Do you read them? How long do they take to complete? Is there a quicker way to get the information you need? Have you asked the people who complete them how they could be improved?

What your team need to be motivated

☐ A strategy that they buy into

☐ Clear job descriptions so they know their contribution to the strategy

☐ Transparent performance measures – am I doing a great job?

☐ Fair remuneration

☐ Adequate resources

☐ Reasonable deadlines

☐ Skills development, particularly training on new systems

☐ Shared, genuine values

☐ Efficient systems and processes – the simpler the better

☐ Psychological safety – a manager that has your back

☐ Space to think without interruption.

Tick those off, then get out of people's way to let them do their best work, go home at a reasonable time and return happy and fresh the next day. It's that simple.

Now that you've cleared the path, the next step to building productive teams is to build trust: psychological safety.

CHAPTER 20

Performance comes from trust

• • •

- Do your team feel that you always have their back?
- Are you consistent or do you have favourites?
- Do you think it's clever to be sarcastic?
- Do your actions match your words?

In 2015, Google published the results of a two-year study into what makes a great team successful. Hiring the best brains, setting them clear objectives and giving them meaningful work were obviously key, but the factor at the very top of the list may surprise you. It was psychological safety. You need to build this within your team if you want them to perform well and be productive.

> *Psychological safety is 'a belief that one will not be punished or humiliated for speaking up with ideas, questions, concerns or mistakes.'*
>
> *Amy Edmondson, Harvard Business School*

Like Google, Amy Edmondson (who developed the concept) found that teams which made more mistakes were actually more successful. Creating an environment in which people feel comfortable to take risks and occasionally mess up is key to fostering innovation and, ultimately, higher performance. Managers want people to step out of their comfort zone. To do that they have to trust that they won't get punished for making mistakes or highlighting possible icebergs. Not only will they not be punished, they are positively encouraged to step up and speak up.

Here's how to build a climate of psychological safety in your team:

1. **Open communication channels:** Stay tuned in to your team's progress with regular check-ins (not check-ups), so people know you will listen to them if they have a problem. When you have a moment, walk round the floor and ask, 'How's it going?' Encourage people to take responsibility and to talk through where they are at with their work. Really listen to them, rather than just waiting to talk yourself. Ask yourself if your point is essential or if you can keep it to yourself. You usually can. You are building their trust, not your ego.

2. **Never mock or be cynical:** Genuinely encourage ideas and never criticize quirky contributions in meetings. Sarcastic comments like 'that's certainly one idea, any others?' gets cheap laughs but shuts down creativity and trust. Be open to ideas that don't match your own.

3. **Set a meeting etiquette:** Meetings are where psychological safety is really on display. Set respectful boundaries – everyone's voice is heard, we look at the person speaking (my bugbear), we don't interrupt each other, no phones.

4. **Deal with problems head on:** Don't shy away from bad news. Get as much accurate information as possible, analyse the causes, fix the problem and collectively change the process moving forward. Show the team how to learn from failure and look for learnings. Our best times at work are when we are overcoming challenges and learning.

5. **Don't get personal – it's about work not personalities:** Don't have favourites, share gossip or be overtly political. Focus on the delivery of work to the highest possible standards and people's contribution. Be objective. Give feedback on behaviours and performance, not traits.

6. **Acknowledge your own mistakes and vulnerabilities:** Lead by example here, as ever. You are fallible too. Ask: 'Can you just double-check the facts for me so I don't miss anything?' 'What am I not seeing now that will be obvious by the end of the project?' 'What are my blind spots on this?'

Here's how not to do it:

When I had my very first job in recruitment, I was sent off for training to the head office with two other newbies. When we returned to our own office, our manager was quite literally waiting at the doorway, ready to berate us for 'admitting there were things you didn't know'. 'Never, ever, do that again', she spat, clearly having already been called and reprimanded about our knowledge gaps. Two weeks into the job and the trust was gone for good. They spent a fortune on international conferences, company cars and incentives but if they'd simply developed a climate of open-ness they'd have got way more effort out of us.

CHAPTER 21

Reclaim the workplace for, like, actual work

• • •

- Is your office too noisy to concentrate in? Or too quiet for you to confidently make a phone call?
- How much time do you get without interruptions?
- Is this an opportunity for you to redesign how you work?

For years, leadership teams have been convinced that creating fun, collegiate, open plan cultures was the key to employee satisfaction and, therefore, productivity.

I visit offices with sport/music/news playing in the background, with endless distractions and open plan layouts where people constantly interrupted each other. Funky snacks everywhere.

They chat but don't talk. Have you ever received a message from the person opposite you asking if you have received the email that they sent you five minutes before? Bonkers.

The five-day-a-week routine may be a thing of the past but we have to set up physical office spaces to make them easier to focus.

Some organizations have tried to encourage reflection, with quieter break-out areas or pods. People tell me that they feel guilty about using them. It feels indulgent.

We are 'knowledge workers', required to think for a living. Probably with some specialist expertise. How nuts is it that we have no Head Space just to think? Figure that one out!

I'm not saying that we should go back to the hierarchical days of the bullpen and corner office but the way we work now isn't working. We have become all yang (noise, passion, drive, aggression) and no yin (space to grow, be calm, restore).

All play and no work

The benefits that come with open plan 'culture', like smoothies, table-tennis, beers, music and workplace yoga are all just hygiene factors. Building a community at work is important but it's not a substitute for good management. You have to manage the workflow. You might sit opposite your team members, but do you actually know what they are doing or how well they are doing it?

We've got the 'play hard' bit cracked. Getting 'work hard' done has become a problem. If you don't believe me, ask people how easy it is to achieve their daily priorities.

As we've seen, one of the basic tenets of increasing productivity is providing the space to do daily, deep Flow working – both for you and for the people that work for you. We don't need to create a festival experience of trance music, shamanic rituals or other mind-altering states. However, you've got to create space to allow people to get into Flow at work, not just at home.

Flow is impossible in a noisy, open plan environment with continual interruptions and multiple digital channels.

Social distancing measures give us an opportunity to redesign our workplaces.

I'm not asking you to nail up partitions but there are interventions that leadership can take to create space so that the workplace is easier to actually work in.

Kombucha on tap or virtual musical bingo sessions will not fix productivity or engagement problems. They are just an amusing diversion. The solution is clarity of objectives, skills development, proper systems and processes. Then a clear path to allow people to achieve them without distractions. It's your responsibility, as a manager, to make this space and clarity happen. Assume everyone starts their day intending to do a good job. Remove everything that stops them from doing it. Frankly you might need to grow a backbone to do this, but they'll thank you for it. You're their manager, so get managing. Suggest they put their phones away for starters. Blame me if you have to.

Remember Teresa Amabile's research? Your team come to work to make incremental progress towards their goals. Period. Provide that and you have motivated, engaged, happy, healthy, productive people. Get them to come to work, do a good job and go home. The more people can re-energize, have hobbies, lives and relationships, the better their creativity and performance will be. Economists say we need to be out spending our money too.

What needs to change?

We've looked at how our work will be activity driven in future, now that it is much more acceptable to work remotely. People will come into work to communicate with each other.

Build co-worker support systems: eating together, talking about how to improve processes, doing pre- and post-mortems, building in planning time, asking for support and advice.

Clear the path of anything that stops people doing great work and having meaningful lives. That includes poorly executed conferences and strategic offsites.

I earn a large proportion of my income talking about Crazy Busyness at conferences, so I am at the sharp end of giving organizations value for money.

How many conferences have you been to that were a complete waste of time? You might have swopped a few business cards, but that's about it.

If you are planning an offsite and taking your team away from their desks, and their families, then make every minute count.

Make your offsites sticky.

The onus is on me, as a speaker, and the conference organizers, to drive real, sustained results – 'sticky' outcomes that will have an on going impact. 'Be inspirational' or 'liven them up after lunch' are do-able but won't really justify the cost of my invoice, or more importantly, taking people away from their day to day operations.

Nail down clear objectives. I always get my client to tell me exactly what changes they want to see as a consequence of my talk, and how that fits in to the theme of the event. Something like reduced bottle necks, clearer communication, increasing innovation, or how we execute the new strategic objectives just outlined by the CEO. The theme has to be clearly communicated before the event.

The work mustn't stop after the event either. There must be a follow-up plan to ensure that changes are tracked and maintained, and someone has to drive that plan. If not, the benefits of getting together can quickly dissipate when people get back to real life.

If you don't have time to plan a really powerful off-site, then host regular team pow-wows instead, with or without an external speaker. These are really effective if you get everyone's voice heard, address one issue at a time and encourage solutions from the front line.

You can use your conference budget to hire a stellar Executive Assistant to do your admin, freeing up more Head Space and leadership time.

Finally choose team 'bonding' events judiciously. As one of my clients said, 'a day out paintballing won't solve my problems. It will just make me better at paintballing.'

CHAPTER 22

Spot the red flags of burnout

• • •

- Do you feel 'used up' at the end of the day?
- Are you feeling increasingly cynical and critical?
- Do you take all your annual leave?
- How often do you check your emails on holiday?
- Were you secretly disappointed not be picked in a redundancy or furlough exercise?

We should all be alert to early signs of burnout in ourselves or our colleagues. Burnout happens at the extreme end of Crazy Busyness. Even when we think we are cured of it, our old busy habits can creep up on us when we are under pressure and take over.

What is burnout?

Burnout is a 'state of vital exhaustion'. It's when we feel overwhelmed, exhausted, mentally and physically tired.

Some of my clients have workloads that are consistently unsustainable. It's only the prospect of their holidays that keep them going during the year. Is this a way to live?

Here's why not. Stress kills. Those endorphin and dopamine hits when you work in Flow or cross tasks off a list are great for you. Continuous stress in your life isn't. It really does eat up your time.

Research published in the Journal of Psychological Ageing concluded that men who experience persistently moderate or high levels of stressful life events over a number of years have a 50 per cent higher mortality rate. They studied almost 1,000 middle-class and working-class men for an 18-year period, from 1985 to 2003. All the men were in good health when they signed up.

In general, the researchers found only a few protective factors against these higher levels of stress – people who self-reported that they had good health tended to live longer and married men also fared better (they didn't check in to see how their wives were doing). Moderate drinkers also lived longer than non-drinkers.

This was the first study to show a direct link between stress and higher mortality rates. Those in the low-stress group experienced an average of two or fewer major life events in a year, compared with an average of three for the moderate group and up to six for the high stress group.

One of the study's most surprising findings was that the mortality risk was similar for the moderate versus high stress group. More than three stress events a year was a problem.

As we age, there are inevitably stressful events in our lives: children, financial responsibilities, elderly parents, our own health worries. Some of us are more anxious and prone to a stress response than others.

Curing your Crazy Busyness will help you to avoid, or at least cope better, with predictable stressful events.

Can you reduce your own stress triggers?

How many potentially stressful periods a year do you have because of your work? There'll be unpredictable curveballs, but are there also events you can mitigate against? Make a note of them here.

_____

_____

_____

_____

_____

_____

_____

_____

_____

_____

Do you make them extra stressful because of the high demands
you put on yourself? Write your thoughts here.

_____

_____

_____

_____

_____

_____

_____

_____

What could you do to make them less stressful? For example:
improved planning, better workflow management, earlier stakeholder communication, improved collaboration and delegation?

_____

_____

_____

_____

_____

_____

_____

_____

IS IT DEPRESSION OR BURNOUT?

How do you know if you are exhausted with work or actually
depressed? A depressed person will take their black dog with them
wherever they go. Burnout, on the other hand, is confined to work. Get
away from your desk (and your boss) and up a mountain, on a beach,
or wherever you can to decompress, and your energy and mood will
be restored.

To state the obvious, people should *not* burn out, take a break, return
to work and repeat the pattern (although I know some who do). That's
madness from any angle: career, psychological, physical or family.

HOW TO SPOT BURNOUT

Here are two canaries in the burnout coalmine:

Burnout Sign #1: Reduced productivity

Your high-performing piece of expensive talent ceases to deliver. It might be you, or a team member. They work even longer hours, but the standard of their tasks tails off. Talk to them about it. Say that you have noticed the changes and ask what they think is going on. It could be that they are just bored and need more responsibilities. Or they could be overwhelmed by their workload and their own relentless drive to excel. Those are predictors of burnout. Coach them to manage the demands of their role and the pressure they put on themselves.

Burnout Sign #2: Cynicism

This varies from an increasingly apathetic approach to the job, when people fall prey to office and digital distractions, to downright pessimism about the impact of their work.

You'll hear previously positive people make snidey comments about the customers, other team members, other departments, or senior management:

- *'What's the point anyway, nothing changes around here?'*
- *'I don't mind teaching, it's just the parents and the children that spoil it.'*
- *'Not him again, what does he want this time?'*

It's sort of funny in the moment, but it's not actually. Negativity and disengagement will drive more motivated team members away. It's certainly not enabling a collaborative culture that screams service, success and energy.

What can you do to prevent burnout happening and restore resilience?

Burnout prevention strategies

RESTORE THE BOUNDARIES

As I keep saying, people are happiest and most motivated when they make daily, incremental progress towards their goals. That's all it takes!

Allow them to get their meaningful work done – with clear role descriptions, targets, performance metrics, deadlines, training and all the resources they need.

Get in your lawn mower, clear the path for them to do great work and then get out of their way.

FAKING IT DOESN'T ALWAYS MAKE IT

I've explained how we can make our mood irrelevant by just getting on with the task and that sometimes making ourselves smile can help us to feel a bit more motivated. However, consistently faking positive emotions, called 'surface acting', is harmful (Hochschild).

A worn-out coffee server, forcing themselves to smile at the customer and keep their own emotions hidden, has an increased risk of burnout and is likely plotting his or her escape. I've seen this often with human resources professionals and also clients in not-for-profit, mission-driven environments like international development. They are busy caring for everyone else, burdened by everyone's problems and not taking care of their own needs and emotions. Get your boundaries back. Self-care is essential.

Isolation and burnout

During COVID-19, so many people experienced that their normally positive mood was fluctuating. This can be partly alleviated by understanding what is and isn't under our control, but also by just moving around and getting away from our screen to get some energy back. Even shifting to a different chair, or standing for a call, can make a difference.

I felt at risk of burnout myself, for the first time ever, in August 2020, working from home (living at work really) during COVID-19. It was relatively minor, but the cheep of the warning canary was a real wake-up call. I was unusually Crazy Busy (sweet irony there).

I've fed a lot of information into the hopper on this over the years, so I should have known better than to neglect my safety nets, social connections particularly. I am an extrovert, which means I get an energy boost from being with other people. Introverts restore their energy with some quiet times to themselves. (It is nothing to do with where you are to be found at a party: starting the dancing or doing the washing-up. That's a misconception.)

Wherever you are on the introversion/extroversion scale, social relationships are what keep all of us going. The secret to joy and energy is as simple as that. Professor Robert Waldinger's work at the Harvard Study of Adult Development proves it. Studies over 80 years showed that close relationships, more than money, fame, possessions or job titles, are what keep people happy throughout their lives. These ties protect us from life's discontents, help to delay mental and physical decline, and are better predictors of long and happy lives than social class, IQ, or even genes. That finding proved true across the board among both the Harvard men surveyed and the inner-city participants.

That's yet another reason why working from home in isolation, despite the gains from the zero commute, isn't good for us. It's possible to feel isolated even if holed up with your large family. We have to actively mitigate against the feeling by doubling-down on social strategies.

Anyway, back to me!

At the time, my client load was particularly demanding. Everyone was navigating the stresses of remote working and keeping their own shows on the road. Grateful for the work, and wanting to help, giving out loads of energy as we do in my job, (yup, defaulting under pressure to my latent co-dependence), I over-extended.

One day, my brain just seemed to stop working. I was trying to read a document, hardly the Northern Irish Peace Protocol, but I still couldn't take in a word. The words swam in front of me and I couldn't focus. That was pretty scary for a control freak like me – had dementia hit already, was this permanent, how was I going to earn a living if my brain was all fogged up? My irrational brain cantered off, catastrophizing. I was somatizing: my stress was manifesting itself with physical symptoms.

I cleared the decks and made myself take a couple of days off. Then I rearranged my work, spreading coaching and speaking sessions more evenly in my calendar, with more gaps to prepare properly in between. I turned down a contract I didn't really want to get involved in. That felt particularly great. Even if it was the 'wrong' decision in financial terms, it put me back in the driving seat.

I reminded myself of what was important to me. 'Earning as much as I can whilst hoping know one spots that I am doing a shit job' isn't one of my values.

I'm exceptionally lucky. I work for myself and I know how to turn things round quickly. Thank goodness for my dog, friends, family (in no particular order, obviously). It's much harder to prioritize self-care when your organization pivots on presenteeism and profits.

Leaders: Walk the talk

If you manage others, you are a role model for both high and healthy performance. You have to take care of yourself and spot when others are over-extended too. If you are locked in endless meetings, snapping at people because you've no time to talk to them, over-promising and under-delivering and working stupid hours, then you've no time to step back and listen to what's happening to yourself or your team.

You need some calm Head Space to think strategically and nip problems in the bud before they escalate. Don't wait for a sickness note or resignation in your team, keep an eye out for those canaries.

MANAGING STRESS

If people are stressed, then find out what their stress trigger is so you can help them develop strategies to cope. Dr Stephen Palmer, an expert in stress management, says stress occurs 'when the perceived pressure exceeds your perceived ability to cope'. Note the word 'perceived'. We vary in our perception of how well we can cope with different stressors. I'm calm in a real crisis but freak out over petty dramas like someone using up the last of the milk. 'I'm not respected, no one supports me, don't they know how hard I work, I'm not in control' – blah blah. Irrational, but a stress trigger, nevertheless.

Our minds can create stress with unhelpful beliefs. Imposter syndrome, that feeling that we aren't good enough, can make manageable tasks feel much more onerous.

Working environments can create stress too. Lousy managers make unreasonable demands and don't give us the right tools to do our job.

Which is it? Labelling these issues under the catch-all 'stress' won't solve the real problem. It just puts a sticky plaster on the symptoms. The issues will still be there when the person returns to work. It also implies that the worker is somehow at fault: not resilient enough, can't cope with pressure. An unspoken black mark.

FIX THE DISEASE, NOT THE SYMPTOM

Talk to your colleague to help them pinpoint the real problem. What's the trigger that makes them feel stressed?

Give them support to help them cope with it. Do they need more time, training, supervision? A Head Space audit might help unpack the problem – perhaps they are trying to do too much in too little time.

ARE YOU THE PROBLEM?

I meet too many managers who *create* stress. Someone said, at a Crazy Busy event, that the only creative thing their Creative Director did was create email chains. It's not funny is it?

Just to remind you of the absolute basics of lawn mower management, if you are working backwards through this book:

- Get proper training on the granular details of managing workflow.

- Only hold meetings that are absolutely necessary, keep to an agenda and don't let anyone waffle.

- Delegate, manage upwards, push back, re-negotiate and say no. All of these are crucial yet basic leadership skills.

- Don't send out of hours emails (save them in your draft folder or use the timed sending facility if you really must write them), or finesse tasks that don't need finessing (that PowerPoint deck is just fine).

HOW DO YOU GET YOUR JUICE UP?

No one can be *on* all the time or in front of a screen. 100,000 years of human existence has not prepared us to live that way. We are built to move and connect, to be productive, not static.

Do less but think more – you'll be more valuable that way. You rarely get your best ideas in the office. Get your 'juice up', as yoga instructor Tania Brown calls it. Encourage your people to take their holidays. Exercise. Breathe. Find a hobby or a challenge outside work that nourishes you. Take a real lunch break and eat with your team or family. Talk. Don't email. Move around. Find a self-care strategy that works for you and PIMP it in your diary, your health should be your number one priority.

CHAPTER 23

Crazy Busy bullying

● ● ●

- Does your manager make excessive demands on your time: calling you at 7.00 am from their car, sending you late-night emails, setting weekend deadlines, and generally trampling over your work–life boundaries?
- Do you suspect that the crazy busy responsibilities you have been given are some sort of weird resilience test?
- Are you nervous of raising your concerns because you tread on eggshells around your manager?

Most of the steps to cure Crazy Busyness are well within our own control: prioritization, organization, assertiveness, discipline.

This chapter is for people who suspect there's something else going on, something insidious. Often they feel that they are the problem, not the person making unreasonable demands, so they don't talk about it. Read on. If this strikes a chord with you, take action. Like all abuse, it's difficult to remove yourself from the situation but you really must.

Is your Crazy Busy schedule imposed on you?

If you raised it with your manager, instead of having a constructive conversation about increasing productivity, would you be criticized and belittled? If so, it is likely that you are a victim of workplace abuse.

This chapter is for you.

Here's how this often plays out:

You joined an organization to work for an amazingly charismatic, high-achieving and powerful leader. They made you feel special, making great efforts to get you on board and sharing their ambitious vision for the future with you. You were flattered, even a little surprised, and hoped that some of their radiance would rub off on you.

Everything is fine to start, but once you get your feet properly under the table, you have a hunch that something is going wrong. You can't put your finger on exactly what. It is difficult to explain this feeling to anyone else without sounding paranoid, but it starts to eat you up.

- Their mood becomes unpredictable and you don't know how they will respond to you. You don't want to upset them with bad news.

- You feel they are never satisfied with your work; that it's never quite good enough. You can't improve it because they won't give you feedback on what they want you to do differently.

- There are some occasions when you know your ideas are on the right track but only because your manager takes the credit for them. If you point this out, they turn on you, accusing you of being over-sensitive or not being a team player.

- They fuss over the newest member of the team and, at the same time, start to devalue the work you do, perhaps in public.

- They make unreasonable demands on your time, expecting you to attend too many meetings and to be available 24/7.

- They blame others for their own mistakes. They have extreme feelings about other people too – they are either flawless or written off as useless/evil/enemies. People are either with them, or against them. Leavers who resign from their team are ostracized. You feel guilty if you stay in touch with them.

- They remember situations and conversations in a different way to how they occurred, rewriting history. You start to question yourself, repeatedly thinking 'is this me?'

- They start to cold-shoulder you, cutting you out of projects and taking you off the list for valuable meetings and emails.

- If challenged, they deny it and roundly criticize your behaviour, even suggesting that you are bullying them. This is classic gas-lighting behaviour.

- Everyone else appears to idolize him or her, constantly praising them. You fear you are going a little crazy.

- You take time off sick, which is unusual for you. I hear most about muscular pains, migraines and digestive problems but stress manifests in many ways.

- You find it hard to move on, because you crave their validation. You hope that, one day, you'll get it if you keep on trying to please them.

- Over time, your shame increases as your self-esteem declines. You wonder what happened to the go-getting, ambitious, positive person you used to be.

It's not you!

If this sounds familiar, then know that they are the problem, not you. You are most likely working for a Narcissistic Boss. Narcissistic Personality Disorder (NPD) is more prevalent in males than females, but there are female narcissists too.

This situation is more common than people realize, because they are too ashamed to talk about it. I've coached many people on surviving narcissistic managers. Even after they escape, the toxicity can continue to impact their careers and confidence until they unpack what happened and rebuild their boundaries.

NPD is thought to occur in less than one per cent of the general population. As highly functioning narcissists are often successful and ambitious, it is not uncommon for them to be in senior leadership or entrepreneurial roles. Most won't have a formal diagnosis, but lack of self-awareness and empathy are hallmarks.

Obviously, many of us have some healthy narcissistic tendencies. They enable us to push ourselves forward and survive corporate life. However, working for a true narcissist can put you in an extremely unpleasant, emotionally abusive relationship. If you have experienced this, you will know exactly what I mean.

What you can do about it:

1. **Try not to take things personally.** One of the consequences of this kind of relationship is that we often feel we are to blame. It triggers our shame or imposter syndrome, which might be lurking not too far from the surface anyway. It won't be the first time that things have played out this way with him/her. There will undoubtedly be

other people who have had similar experiences with them. If you look closely enough you will realize that the narcissist doesn't really have close relationships; merely people that hang round them, flattering them to achieve their own ends. The really strong ones move on sooner or later.

2. **Keep up the pretence.** Never let them know you have seen through the mask. They rarely change, so you have to change your response to them. Narcissists have a strong vision of who they think they should be and are controlled by their shame of not living up to this ideal. Bursting their bubble is the worst thing you can do. Their response to any challenge will be aggressive and vengeful. Instead, let them live up to their false view of themselves. Keep the image going by stroking their ego as much as you can bear. This is for your own self-preservation. Best of all, encourage them to move onwards and upwards. You might be surprised at the allies you have in this. How many times do we see this happen? People get promoted out of the way, to become someone else's problem.

3. **Take responsibility for your own behaviour.** Co-dependents are people who allow themselves to be controlled or manipulated by others. They are natural magnets for narcissists. Narcissists can't survive without people to feed their ego and co-dependents give up their own needs to fuel the needs of the narcissist. A perfect match. If you have a tendency to put others' needs before your own, always trying to fix things for them and wanting to please, then you are displaying co-dependent behaviour. This makes you the natural other half in the narcissist relationship. You may have had similar relationship patterns earlier in your life.

4. **Get out of it.** Even if you successfully use these tactics, working for a narcissist will make you feel isolated, stressed and anxious. None of these are good for you, your career or your other relationships. Carefully consider whether you want to continue working for this person, particularly if their behaviour appears to be escalating. If they remain a popular figure in the organization – or one not to be crossed – your concerns might not be taken as seriously as they should be. Sending you off on sick leave with 'stress' solves nothing but I see this happen often in these circumstances. You are not sick! You are being emotionally abused. Sick leave cures the symptoms, not the disease.

What you must never do

Do not challenge them. The usual advice on dealing with bullies won't work with a narcissist. It will escalate their abuse. Remember they have no empathy, so they don't care how their behaviour makes you feel. All they care about is how good you make them look. Your misery actually makes them feel better.

The only way to save your sanity and career is to get away from them. Start to take care of yourself, not everyone else. You will be so much happier.

HR: You have a ticking time bomb

If you employ one of these managers, then understand that their behaviour is likely to get nastier. You won't be able to ignore it for much longer. It's rare to get honest feedback on them because people are frightened of repercussions. There will be clues to spot, not least your retention figures. Find a reason to move them out before they do even more damage to your culture and reputation. If you really can't afford to lose their positive aspects (like business development strengths), shift them back to an individual contributor role. They can be hailed as a Captain Fantastic for bringing in results without hurting other people.

PART 5

Freedom

CHAPTER 24

If you aren't a Crazy Busy person anymore, who are you?

• • •

- What are you going to do with the time you've saved?
- If you aren't describing yourself as 'Crazy Busy' anymore, what are you instead?
- Your own agenda is now top of your list; what's on it?

Crazy Busy is no longer your badge of honour. You've ditched a way of thinking and behaving that's no longer useful to you. You've taken agency of your own life, choosing what you do and when you do it. That's my definition of success.

Does a hamster know what to do when you take him off the wheel?

Millions long for immortality who do not know what to do with themselves on a rainy Sunday afternoon.

Susan Ertz

If you aren't Crazy Busy anymore, who are you?

Crazy Busy people are sensitive high achievers beneath the veneer. We worry about others' perceptions of us and whether we are good enough. We are control-freaks too. We want to control everything, and everyone, to help us feel secure. That's why we become so successful, but at the expense of our own mental health and desires. We subjugate our own wishes to other people's, giving away our power.

When we work through the steps of the cure, and claw back the time lost through organizational drag, we learn to build boundaries. We start to make a more active choice about what we do all day. We prioritize our own agenda, not everyone else's. We know what we want, and we ask for it. We worry less about making everyone happy because we know it's impossible.

Getting in control of how we spend our time is wonderfully liberating. We live much closer to our values and become more successful too. But please expect to feel vulnerable as you change. Filling the day with distracting small stuff is a great excuse. It stops us from dwelling on our real challenges or facing up to the gaps in our lives. Being a victim of busyness gets us out of scary situations. 'I can't speak at the conference, I've just got too much on.' Rushing is a great distraction from who we really are and what we really need.

I had one client who felt so disconnected from his young children that he stopped trying to get home for their bed-time, blaming the demands of his job. I have plenty more who spend their weekends working and exercising excessively, rather than slowing down and risking the rough and tumble of a truly connected life. Who hasn't got out of parties by pretending to be exhausted by work, rather than risk social rejection? I know I'm guilty of that.

We won't have the abundance of success and love we deserve if we blank-out our real feelings and needs with busyness.

To paraphrase Daring Greatly author and TED talk sensation Dr Brené Brown, busyness is a great numbing strategy, and one that many of us are very familiar with. Through her work, Brown calls for us to get to know our own needs and desires and to allow ourselves to be vulnerable.

Curing crazy busyness means facing up to our real selves. Stop comparing yourself to other people and create time for the work and activities that give you an abundance of success and happiness.

What do you really need?

What *do* you really need?

I don't want you to do 'less', just more of what you need.

You still have 168 hours in the week, as Laura Vanderkam spells out in her book: *168 Hours: You Have More Time Than You Think.* That title says it all. More than you thought, eh?

What are you going to do with your time now? You might spend the same amount of time at work, making better choices about how you spend it.

I just want you to do less of the wrong things and do more of the things that keep you happy, successful and fulfilled.

Freedom from the burden of Crazy Busyness

I want you to:

- Switch off, then switch on again whole-heartedly so you aren't stressing yourself out trying to endlessly multi-task.
- Stick to your own job, not be busy micromanaging other people's work, or doing their work for them because that way it'll be done right. Not everything has to be perfect.
- Find time to develop people, to look at people when they speak and really make them feel valued and special, so they feel great about themselves.
- Think, to find Head Space to innovate, be creative, find solutions to complex problems and do your very best work when it counts.

Stop sleepwalking into unhealthy, unproductive and damaging habits by not taking stock of how you spend your time. What an outlier you would be in most organizations if your colleagues, and loved ones, felt you really listened to them, so they wanted to think through their issues with you in order to reach their own solution.

Most of all, I want you to take the time to fall back in love with what you do and find the meaning in your work, not in the busyness of it.

Time isn't just money.

I've talked a lot about the economic value of time: the investment cost of switching tasking, the wasted time through organizational drag and how businesses squander their highly paid talent by not clearing the path in front of them.

Time is more than a resource that we can't replace. It also has a significant personal value.

Please don't sacrifice your precious years on work that doesn't matter or pointless email conversations or other people's urgent and selfish demands.

It is a privilege to be busy with work and life, but it is time to replace the competitively, out of control, craziness. Choose to be wonderfully, happily, purposefully, focused, connected busy and efficient instead.

The world has changed since COVID-19. Organizations can track productivity in many ways now that are much less offensive than Taylor's stopwatch. We know that in many cases output has improved. But what about input, how we nurture and look after ourselves? For many, Crazy Busyness has boiled over as the boundaries between work and home have become indistinguishable. Busyness temporarily takes our mind off scary external forces, but it is an unhealthy survival strategy.

Start again tomorrow – and that email can wait until then too.

I hope this book prompts you to make sustainable changes that impact on your life, the people you work with and your loved ones too.

It's time to change your narrative too and reinvent yourself. Find your true game-changer. It takes courage to put yourself out there and take a risk, so plan the first step. And take it!

Next time someone asks you how you are, what will you say?

Please let me know: <zena@zenaeverett.com>.

Sign up for my monthly article to help you stay cured – it's an antelope, I promise: <www.zenaeverett.com>.

References

Aristotle, *Politics*, translated by A. M. William Ellis (2015) CreateSpace Independent Publishing Platform.

Introduction

Wansink, B. (2006), *Mindless Eating: Why We Eat More Than We Think*, New York: Bantam Books.

Holt-Lunstad J., Smith T.B., Baker M., Harris T., Stephenson D., (March 2015), 'Loneliness and social isolation as risk factors for mortality: a meta-analytic review'. Perspect Psychol Sci. 2015 Mar;10(2):227–37. doi: 10.1177/1745691614568352. PMID: 25910392.

Mankins, M., Garton, E. (2017), *Time, Talent, Energy, Overcome Organizational Drag and Unleash Your Team's Productive Power*, Boston, MA: Harvard Business Review Press.

Dahlgreen, W. (2015) '37% of British workers think their jobs are meaningless', YouGov, available at: <yougov.co.uk/topics/lifestyle/articles-reports/2015/08/12/british-jobs-meaningless> (accessed December 2020).

Chapter 1

Goldsmith, M. (2008), *What Got You Here Won't Get You There*, London: Profile Books.

Richardson, K. and Norgate, S.H. (2015) 'Does IQ really predict job performance?' *Applied Developmental Science*, 19(3): 153–169.

Cast, C. (2018) *The Right and Wrong Stuff: How Brilliant Careers are Made and Unmade*, New York: Public Affairs.

Beattie, M. (1986) *Codependent No More: How to Stop Controlling Others and Start Caring for Yourself*, Center City, MN: Hazelden Publishing.

Chapter 2
Cast, C. (2018) *The Right and Wrong Stuff: How Brilliant Careers are Made and Unmade*, New York: Public Affairs.

Chapter 4
Dillard, A. (1989) *The Writing Life*, New York: Harper Perennial.

Dweck, C. (2017) *Mindset – Changing the Way you Think to Fulfil Your Potential*, London: Robinson.

Whitmore, J. (2002) *Coaching for Performance*, London: John Murray Press.

Camerer, C. et al. (1997) 'Labor Supply of New York City Cabdrivers: One Day at a Time' *Quarterly Journal of Economics*, 112: 407–41.

Burkeman, O. (2012) *The Antidote: Happiness for People Who Can't Stand Positive Thinking*, London: Canongate Books Ltd.

Chapter 5
Campari, G. et al., (2016) *The 99 Essential Business Questions To Take You Beyond the Obvious Management Actions*, Croydon: Filament Publishing Ltd.

Ferriss, T. (2007) *The 4-Hour Workweek: Escape 9-5, Live Anywhere, and Join the New Rich*, New York: Crown Publishing Group.

Chapter 6
Zeigarnik, B. (1938) 'On Finished and Unfinished Tasks', in W. D. Ellis (Ed.), *A Sourcebook of Gestalt Psychology* (pp. 300–314), London: Kegan Paul, Trench, Trubner & Co.

Draper, D. (2018) *Create Space: How to Manage Time and Find Focus, Productivity and Success*, London: Profile Books.

Chapter 7
Ofcom (2018) Communications Market Report, available from: <www.ofcom.org.uk/__data/assets/pdf_file/0022/117256/CMR-2018-narrative-report.pdf>

Ophir E., Nass C. and Wagner A.D. (2009) 'Cognitive control in media multitaskers', *Proceedings of the National Academy of Sciences of the United States of America*, September, 106(37): 15583–15587.

Miller, G.A. (1956) 'The magical number seven, plus or minus two: Some limits on our capacity for processing information', *Psychological Review*, 63(2): 81–97.

Meyer, D.E., Evans, J.E., Lauber, E.J., Rubinstein, J., Gmeindl, L., Junck, L. and Koeppe, R.A. (1997) 'Activation of brain mechanisms for executive mental processes in cognitive task switching', *Journal of Cognitive Neuroscience*, Vol. 9.

Chapter 8

Cranston, S. and Keller, S. (January 2013), Increasing the Meaning Quotient at Work, McKinsey Quarterly, available from: <www.mckinsey.com/business-functions/organization/our-insights/increasing-the-meaning-quotient-of-work>

Kotler, S. and Wheal, J. (2017) *Stealing Fire*, New York: HarperCollins Publishers.

Csikszentmihalyi, M. (2008), *Flow: The Psychology of Optimal Experience*, New York: Harper Perennial Modern Classics.

Krznaric, R. (2012) *How to Find Fulfilling Work*, London: The School of Life.

Evans, J. (2017) *The Art of Losing Control: A Philosopher's Search for Ecstatic Experience*, London: Canongate Books Ltd.

Chapter 9

Ofcom (2018) Communications Market Report, available from: https://www.ofcom.org.uk/__data/assets/pdf_file/0022/117256/CMR-2018-narrative-report.pdf

Chapter 10

Chui M. et al. (July 2012) *The Social Economy: Unlocking Value and Productivity Through Social Technologies*, New York: McKinsey Global Institute.

Zhu, M. and Yang, Y. (2018) *The Mere Urgency Effect*, Oxford: Oxford University Press.

Chapter 11

Dorothy Parker quote from Woollcott, A. (1989) *While Rome Burns*, New York: Simon and Schuster Ltd.

Bregman, P. (2011) *18 Minutes to Find Your Focus, Master Distractions & Get The Right Things Done*, London: Orion Books Ltd.

Mark, G., Gonzalez, V. and Harris, J. (2005) No task left behind? Examining the nature of fragmented work, In *Proceedings of the CHI Conference on Human Factors in Computing Systems*, ACM Press, 113–120.

Mark, G., Gudith, D. and Klocke U. (2008) The cost of interrupted work: more speed and stress. In *Proceedings of the CHI Conference on Human Factors in Computing Systems*, ACM Press, 107–110.

Chapter 12

Williams, J. (2018) *Stand Out of Our Light: Freedom and Resistance in the Attention Economy*, Cambridge: Cambridge University Press.

Porter, H. (2016) 'Why cool cats rule the internet', *The Telegraph* online, available at: <https://www.telegraph.co.uk/pets/essentials/why-cool-cats-rule-the-internet/> (accessed December 2020)

Raphael, R. (2017) 'Netflix CEO Reed Hastings: Sleep is our competition', *Fast Company*, available at: <https://www.fastcompany.com/40491939/netflix-ceo-reed-hastings-sleep-is-our-competition?> (accessed December 2020).

Stewart, J.B. (2016) 'Facebook has 50 minutes of your time each day: It wants more', *The New York Times*, 5 May.

dscout (2015) 'Mobile touches, dscout's inaugural study on humans and their tech', June 15 available from: https://blog.dscout.com/mobile-touches

Ward, A.F., Duke, K., Gneezy, A. and Bos, M.W. (2017) 'Brain drain: The mere presence of one's own smartphone reduces available cognitive capacity', *Journal of the Association for Consumer Research*, 2,(2): 140–154.

Chapter 13

Bregman, P. (2011) *18 Minutes to Find Your Focus, Master Distractions & Get The Right Things Done*, London: Orion Books Ltd.

Repenning, N., Kieffer, D. and Repenning, J. (2018) 'A new approach to designing work', *MIT Sloan Management Review*, available at: <sloanreview.mit.edu/article/a-new-approach-to-designing-work/>

Chapter 14

Iyengar, S. (2011) *The Art of Choosing: The Decisions We Make Everyday of our Lives, What They Say About Us and How We Can Improve Them*, London: Abacus.

Chapter 15

Taylor, F.W. (1998 edition), *The Principles of Scientific Management*, New York: Dover Publications Inc.

Gallup, Inc. (2017) *State of the Global Workplace Report*, Washington: Gallup Press.

Locke, E.A. and Latham, G.P. (1990) *A Theory of Goal-Setting and Task Performance*, New Jersey: Prentice Hall.

Reeves, M., Torres, R. and Hassan, F. (2017) 'How to regain the lost art of reflection', *Harvard Business Review*, 25 September.

Chapter 16

ACAS, 'Neurodiversity in the workplace', available at: <archive.acas.org.uk/neurodiversity> (accessed December 2020)

Chapter 17

Doshi, N. and McGregor, L. (2015), *Primed to Perform: How to Build the Highest Performing Cultures Through the Science of Total Motivation*. New York: Harper Business.

Bloom, N., Liang, J., Zhichun, R.J. and Ying, J. (2013) *Does Working from Home Work? Evidence from a Chinese Experiment*, Cambridge, MA: National Bureau of Economic Research.

Chapter 19
Amabile, T. and Kramer, S. (2011) *The Progress Principle: Using Small Wins to Ignite Joy, Engagement and Creativity at Work*, Boston, MA: Harvard Business Press.

Chapter 20
Edmondson, A.C. (2018) *The Fearless Organization: Creating Psychological Safety in the Workplace for Learning, Innovation, and Growth*, New Jersey: Wiley.

Duhigg, C. (2016) *What Google Learned From Its Quest to Build the Perfect Team*, New York: The New York Times.

Chapter 22
Lee H., Aldwin C.M., Choun S. and Spiro A. (2019), 'Impact of combat exposure on mental health trajectories in later life: Longitudinal findings from the VA Normative Aging Study' *Journal of Psychological Ageing, 34(4):467–474.*

Hochschild, A.R. (1983) *The Managed Heart: Commercialization of Human Feeling*, Oakland, CA: University of California Press.

Waldinger, R.J. (2017) 'Over nearly 80 years, Harvard Study has been showing how to live a healthy and happy life', *Harvard Gazette*, 4 November.

Palmer S., Cooper C. and Thomas K. (2003) *Creating a Balance: Managing Stress*, London: British Library.

Tania Brown Yoga <www.taniabrownyoga.co.uk>

Chapter 24
Ertz, S. (1943) *Anger in the Sky*, London: Hodder & Stoughton.

Brown, B. (2012) *Daring Greatly: How the Courage to be Vulnerable Transforms the Way we Live, Love, Parent and Lead*, New York: Avery Publishing Group.

Vanderkam, L. (2019) *168 Hours: You Have More Time Than You Think*, New York: Portfolio.

About the author

Zena Everett is an international leadership coach and speaker on Crazy Busyness.

Originally a recruitment entrepreneur, Zena sold her business in 2007 and studied an MSc in Career Management and Coaching. She then took further post-graduate qualifications in psychological coaching and leadership with neuroscience (MIT Sloan Business School).

She has coached on the Executive MBA Programme and Oxford University's Saïd Business School and is an Associate Lecturer on Crazy Busyness and Guts Brains & High Performance at Henley Business School.

Zena is a regular speaker on Crazy Busyness and Leadership for the London Business Forum: 'the world's best speakers in London's most iconic venues'.

Her first book is the career manual, *Mind Flip: Take the Fear out of Your Career* (Curlew House, 2020).

Zena lives in London and can be reached at: <www.zenaeverett.com>

Book group questions

1. What would you do if you had an extra hour to yourself?
2. Why don't you do enough of this now?
3. How can you create some time to fit this in?
4. What do you do that is most fulfilling?
5. How can you do more of it?
6. Are you a people pleaser? Is this helping you or holding you back?
7. Are you a slave to your to-do list? Or to someone else's?
8. If you weren't crazy busy anymore, what would you like to do instead?
9. What could you stop doing altogether?

Index

mood, 84–6
motivation, 81–6, 92, 94, 107, 122
multitasking, 18, 42–4

Narcissistic Personality Disorder (NPD), 125
Nass, Clifford, 42
negativity, 118
Netflix, 68
neurodivergence, 87–90

Ophir, Eyal, 42
organizational drag, xxiv
organizational skills, 8
overwhelm, 76–7, 92

Palmer, Dr Stephen, 121
Parker, Dorothy, 61
Parkinson's Law, 36, 92
people-pleasing, 6–8, 64
perfectionism, xxi–xxii, 4–5, 20, 77
phones, 59
    vs. emails, 19
    and social media, 67–71
PIMP process, 36–8
planning, priorities, 35–41
Plato, 48, 67
play, in the workplace, 112–14
PowerPoint, 54
prioritization, 18, 35–41, 58
procrastination, xxi–xxii, 72, 77
productivity, 26, 118
progress, facilitating, 106
psychological safety, 108–10

quality over quantity, 9–10

Repenning, Nelson, 75
responsibilities
    caring roles, 6–8
    taking on too many, 5

saying 'no', 64–5
social isolation, 119–20
social media, 67–71
social relationships, xx, 24
Stewart, James B., 69
strengths, shadow side, 3–8
stress, 115–17, 120, 121–2, 125
summary, 18–20
'surgeries', 63

Taylor, Frederick Winslow, 81–2
time
    making to-do lists, 74
    managing interruptions, 62–4
    wasted, xxiv, 69–71
    working hours, 10–11
time management, 9–13
to-do lists, 20, 72–5
trust, 108–10

uncertainty, 27–8
Urgency Effect, 58

value added, 9–10, 32–3
values
    identifying, 21–3
    realising, 23–4
virtual meetings, 56–7

Wagner, Anthony D., 42
Waldinger, Professor Robert, 120

Would you like your people to read this book?

If you would like to discuss how you could bring these ideas to your team, we would love to hear from you. Our titles are available at competitive discounts when purchased in bulk across both physical and digital formats. We can offer bespoke editions featuring corporate logos, customized covers, or letters from company directors in the front matter can also be created in line with your special requirements.

We work closely with leading experts and organizations to bring forward-thinking ideas to a global audience. Our books are designed to help you be more successful in work and life.

For further information, or to request a catalogue, please contact: **business@johnmurrays.co.uk**
sales-US@nicholasbrealey.com (North America only)

Nicholas Brealey Publishing is an imprint of
John Murray Press.